Pyramids of the Fourth Dynasty

Farid Atiya

Pyramids of the Fourth Dynasty
Farid Atiya

Published by Farid Atiya Press
©Farid Atiya Press

P.O. Box 75, 6th of October City, Giza, Cairo, Egypt
www.faridatiyapress.com, e-mail : atiya@link.net
First edition, 2004
Second Reprint, 2004

All photos are by Farid Atiya
Computer drawings by Shady al-Tayyar

Colour Separation by Farid Atiya Press
Printed and bound in Egypt by Farid Atiya Press

Dar al-Kuteb Registration 13092/2003
ISBN 977-17-0944-5

Right & page 5: the Great Sphinx guarding Chephren's Pyramid. The Sphinx has the
form of a seated lion, and its head represents the image of Chephren wearing the
nemes.

Page 4: the Great Pyramid of Cheops and the Pyramid of Chephren photographed
from a rock south east. In the foreground is the Sphinx, guardian of the Pyramids. Below are the modern tombs of Nazlet al-Seman village.

Page 6: the western face of the Bent Pyramid at Dahshur. The original limestone casing is the best preserved of all pyramids. This pyramid gives the best idea of the spar-
kling brilliance that the pyramids of Egypt had before their casings were stripped
away. Mostly these casings were removed and used to build Cairo houses.

Page 7: Snefru's Bent Pyramid at Dahshur, viewed from south, in the foreground is a
small satellite pyramid. Far behind is the North or Red Pyramid also belonging to
Snefru.

Preface

In less than a hundred years the Third Dynasty witnessed an immense development in the fields of architecture, arts, agriculture, irrigation and mining. This immense wealth led to the creation of a powerful state ruled by mighty Pharaohs revered by their subjects. This is particularly true of the Pharaohs of the Fourth Dynasty. The emergence of giant-size pyramids is evidence of their wealth and divine status. But still, the main driving force behind pyramid building was strictly religious.

In this rising Egyptian state, each Pharaoh aimed at surpassing his predecessor with achievements that opened doors to Eternity (every Pharaoh's ultimate goal). Djoser and Snefru were great in their own right, but Cheops aimed to exceed them. He said: "My rule will be the greatest and will exceed that of my great father Snefru."

The Pyramid Age lasted about 500 years, from the middle of the twenty-seventh to the middle of the twenty-second century BC. In spite of the short reign of the Pharaohs of the Fourth Dynasty (115 years), their achievements became the emblem of both modern and Ancient Egypt. Modern-day Egyptians are immensely proud of their heritage and maintain strong bonds to their glorious past. The Great Pyramid, the Great Sphinx and the pyramids of Snefru, the diorite statue of Chephren, the Triad statues of Mycerinus, the limestone statue of Ra Hotep and Nofert, the wooden statue of Sheikh al-Balad, the scribes in the Louvre and in the Egyptian Museum are till this day a constant source of human inspiration, having achieved their purpose of eternity. They have, in fact, expressed fully the connection between earthly and divine power.

Describing the pyramids in chronological order will enable the reader to understand the logical evolution of the pyramid as a building with religious connotations. Writing a book on the pyramids is like swimming in the open sea. The subject is so vast and so much has been written about it.

In this book I used my profession as a photographer to produce these pictures. The printing quality is a result of all steps being taken under my supervision; colour separation, image setting, offset printing and binding were all carried out at my printing press "Farid Atiya Press". We included CAD drawings of the Pyramids and illustrated them in isometric representations as well as 'wire' transparent structures showing the inner passages and chambers and their relation to the faces. This we did by drawing 'hyper planes' that coincided with the chambers and passages and intersect the Pyramid's face. To my knowledge, drawing the pyramids in this manner has not appeared in previous literature. I would like to thank architect Shady al-Tayyar for making the computer drawings.

The Great Pyramid was extensively linked to mathematical models in the 19th century. As a mathematician, I tried to explain in a simple way the mathematics of the Great Pyramid. In my opinion this is still a subject of research. The literature on geometry and mathematics in Ancient Egypt shows that the mathematical framework employed was very elementary. However, measurements and surveys of the Great Pyramid show that it could only be achieved by men who had great knowledge in geometry and several vital fields such as engineering, construction, organisation, material properties, mining, etc. In my opinion geometry was born in Ancient Egypt and not in Greece. The architect of the Great Pyramid must have had vast knowledge of geometry. Euclid presented in his book *The Elements* the theory of relative measurements and divine proportions, thus denying the fact that Cheops, who 2,300 years before him had applied these geometrical models to his Great Pyramid. Inner passages of the Great Pyramid have dimensions consisting of integer multiples of their basic measurement unit. Angle of slopes in inner passages were all ratios of integer numbers. For example, the ascending and descending passages have a slope ratio of $2:1$ making an angle of $26°\ 18'\ 9.73''$.

It was not only geometry that was founded in Ancient Egypt, but also engineering and organisation. The eminent Egyptologist Ahmed Fakhry is quoted regarding the construction of the Great Pyramid: "If any special skill has disappeared, it is that of the organisers who supervised the timing of the various operations. The process of quarrying, transporting and erecting these monuments was an ordinary matter for the Ancient Egyptians, and therefore went unrecorded. Most of the knowledge we have is based on the study of the monuments themselves."

Finally, I would like to thank Dr Zahi Hawass for the encouragement I received from him and for giving me permission to photograph the Fourth Dynasty's statues in the Egyptian Museum.

Farid Atiya

Cairo, August 2003

Left: the pyramids of Dahshur viewed from across the lake. From left to right: the Bent Pyramid, the Red Pyramid (both built by Snefru, Fourth Dynasty, *c.* 2600 BC), ruins of Amenemhat's pyramid, XIIth Dynasty.

Drawing of the Giza Pyramids from 'Picturesque, Palestine, Sinai and Egypt'
edited by Colonel Wilson R. E., New York 1883.

Contents

Old Kingdom
Narmer
Palette
3200 BC

SMITING THE ENEMY,
Pharaoh Narmer is repre-
sented as the Pharaoh of both
Upper and Lower Egypt. He
is wearing the tall white
crown of Upper Egypt, and
battles to unite Upper and
Lower Egypt under his rule.
This first Dynasty commemo-
rative palette is one of Egypt's
oldest surviving historical records. It was found in
Hierakonopolis, the ancient
capital of Upper Egypt.

Here the Pharaoh, wearing
the White Crown of Upper
Egypt, smashes with a club
the head of his enemy, probably an inhabitant of Lower
Egypt. This representation became a standard symbol in
Egyptian Art for the next
3,000 years. The Pharaoh here
is also decorated with an animal tail and is followed by his
sandal-bearer. Above the enemy is the Pharaoh incar-
nated as the hawk-god, Horus,
holding the enemy with a rope
with his strong right hand.
The enemy is within the papyrus marches of the Delta. The
hawk symbolises 'the god
Horus', i.e. the divine representation of the Pharaoh, and
the papyrus means Lower
Egypt. One can therefore explain this emblem as Pharaoh
Narmer conquering the Delta.
Two bearded men, enemies of
the Pharaoh, are fleeing naked, possibly running or
swimming, or are, as most see
it, lying dead on the ground.

CELEBRATING TRIUMPH.
Pharaoh Narmer wears the captured Red Crown of Lower Egypt at the top of the palette's reverse side. Four priests, smaller in size, stand in front of him carrying fetishes. The sandal bearers stand behind him. It has been suggested that his being barefoot denotes the strong bond between the Pharaoh and the land. Ten beheaded corpses are lain out as if for inspection, their heads placed between their legs. The fact that these bodies are bound suggests they were executed after falling into Narmer's hands. Mutilation of fallen enemies was commonplace in Pharaonic Egypt. Below him slaves leash two panthers. At the bottom of the palette the Pharaoh as a strong bull attacks an enemy town; its temples and houses are shown. The Pharaoh tramples his enemy.

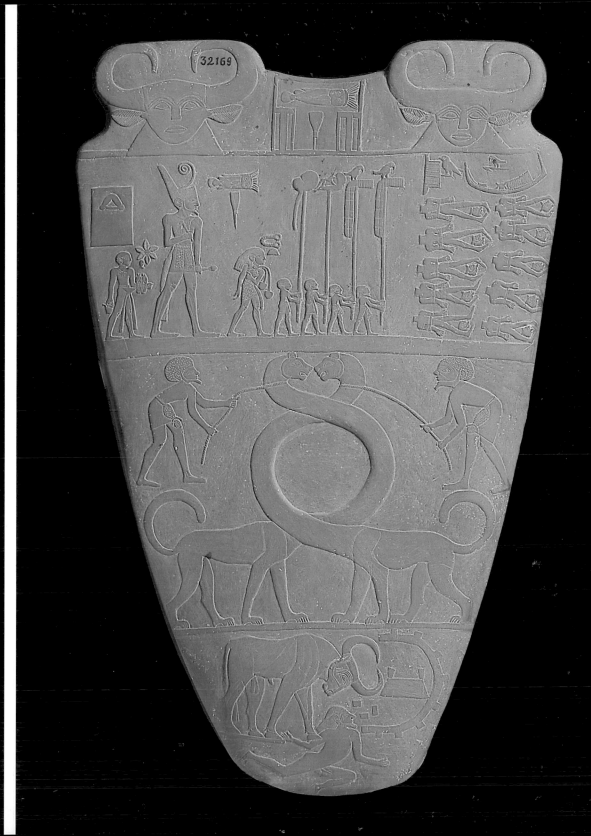

Pyramid Builders in the Third Millennium BC

Djoser 2668 - 2649 BC

Pharaoh Djoser, whose Horus name was Netjerikhe, extended Egypt's southern boundary to Aswan. His most famous achievement was building the Step Pyramid, now regarded as the first large stone building ever raised on earth. The genius who planed this Pyramid was his vizir Imhotep.

Snefru 2613 - 2589 BC

Pharaoh Snefru, the founder of the Fourth Dynasty, came to the throne by marrying Queen Hetepheres, the daughter of Pharaoh Huni. Snefru's mother was a member of Pharaoh Huni's harim. By marrying Huni's daughter, who was also his half-sister, Snefru confirmed by blood legitimacy his right to the throne. He was a legendary figure, and his reign seems to have been glorious. He was considered a kind and beloved Pharaoh, and the cult of Snefru flourished for centuries after his death.

Snefru is the only Pharaoh in Egypt who has four pyramids attributed to him. He completed the Pyramid at Meidum, which had been started by his predecessor Pharaoh Huni. He then built the Bent Pyramid and the Northern Pyramid at Dahshur. Snefru ruled Egypt for over 50 years.

Cheops 2589 - 2566 BC

Khufu, named Cheops in Greek, was the son of Pharaoh Snefru and Queen Hetepheres, the daughter and heiress of Pharaoh Huni. Khnum-khufu, Khufu for short, chose the Giza Plateau in 2589 BC to build his Great Pyramid.

It is not clear how long Cheops's reign lasted. The Turin Canon, written 1,400 years after Cheops's death, states that his reign lasted 23 years, but Manetho wrote that his reign lasted 63 years. Cheops was a charismatic ruler, and in his reign art and building flourished. His son Djedefre succeeded him on the throne.

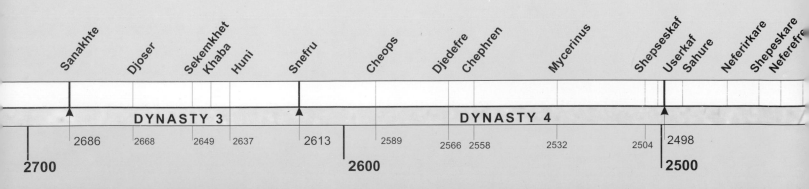

Sanakhte · Djoser · Sekemkhet · Khaba · Huni · Snefru · Cheops · Djedefre · Chephren · Mycerinus · Shepseskaf · Userkaf · Sahure · Neferirkare · Shepeskare · Neferefre

DYNASTY 3   **DYNASTY 4**

2700 — 2686 — 2668 — 2649 — 2637 — 2613 — 2589 — 2566 — 2558 — 2532 — 2504 — 2498 — 2500

Chephren 2558 - 2532 BC

Pharaoh Chephren was the son of Cheops. He succeeded Djedefre, who reigned only briefly. Chephren's reign was considered a restoration of Cheops's traditions. Chephren returned the royal necropolis to Giza where he built his pyramid and valley temple and carved the sphinx.

Mycerinus 2532 - 2504 BC

Pharaoh Mycerinus was the fourth Pharaoh of the Fourth Dynasty, successor of the Pharaoh Chephren, and was known to the Egyptians as Neter-Menkeure, meaning 'Menkeure is Divine'. He was the builder of the Third Pyramid in Giza. The Pharaoh died before the completion of his funerary temple, which was finished by his son Shepseskaf. Mycerinus was a fair and beloved ruler.

Userkaf, 2498 - 2491 BC

Pharaoh Userkaf is the founder of the Fifth Dynasty. He built a small Pyramid, in Sakkara. It is now much in ruins. He also built a sun-temple in Abusir, it was a replica of the sun temple in Heliopolis.

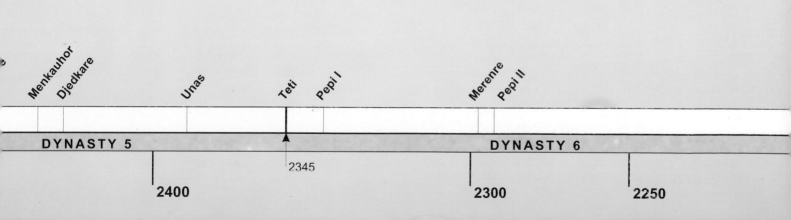

Menkauhor Djedkare Unas Teti Pepi I Merenre Pepi II

DYNASTY 5   **DYNASTY 6**

2345

2400   2300   2250

Introduction

The three Pyramids of Giza are beyond doubt the surpassing expression of Pharaonic majesty and power. They are the sole survivors of the Seven Wonders of the Ancient World. The Giza Pyramids remain so substantial that, when seen from a distance, they seem in ideal geometric form. However, only from a close distance does the wear of time and man's action show. The second pyramid alone retains at its apex some of the original casing of white limestone that once made the slopes of the first two pyramids a mathematically-defined flat surface. Moreover, the rugged, step-like sides of all three pyramids have been attacked by impatient treasure hunters, and also used in the Middle Ages as a quarry for Cairo houses. Yet the three monuments are so huge that they have triumphantly defied human destruction.

The Pyramids of Giza lie south-west of Cairo on a flat elevation of the Western Desert. A walk around the Great Pyramid of Cheops will give a general impression of its huge size and can be followed by a visit to the burial chamber inside. The Sphinx, in the valley below, should be seen next. Tourists who are not pressed for time should hire a camel or a horse at the Great Pyramid and, after visiting the sites, ride into the desert past the Mycerinus and Chephren pyramids. The early morning hours are particularly fresh and pleasant.

The Giza Pyramids are part of the great Cities of the Dead of the Old Kingdom, extending from Abu Rawash in the North to Dahshur in the South. In all, there are six of these pyramid groups, spreading over some 30 kilometres along the eastern edge of the Western Desert plateau.

They are:

1. Abu Rawash, the most northerly.
2. Giza, the biggest (including the Pyramid of Cheops).
3. Zawiyet Aryan, which is mostly in ruins.
4. Abusir.

Left and right: the Giza Pyramids. About 4,700 years ago, Egypt entered an era of great technological progress. Until about 3000 BC, the basic building material was sun-dried brick. About 200 years later the Pyramids of Giza were built of stone blocks, weighing on the average 15 tons each and fitted together with great precision. The techniques of constructing these great monuments were invented by Imhotep, the vizier of Pharaoh Djoser. At Sakkara, using small stone blocks instead of traditional mud bricks, Imhotep built the Step Pyramid and the funerary temple. Nothing similar to these buildings had ever been built on earth.

Top right: drawing of the Giza Pyramids from *Glimpses of the Land of Egypt* by W. H. Bartlett, London, 1850.

5. Sakkara, the oldest (including the Pyramid of Djoser).

6. Dahshur, the southernmost group (including the Bent Pyramid).

There are also pyramids at Lisht, Meidum and Fayoum.

Each of these pyramid groups is the centre of a city of the dead; all round the large pyramids are smaller ones (usually those of queens) and mastabas, the tombs of those nobles who filled high office during the life of the Pharaoh. They are generally buried in proximity to their royal masters, close to whom they desired to remain even after this life. To each pyramid belongs a temple where sacrifices were offered and ritual services were held.

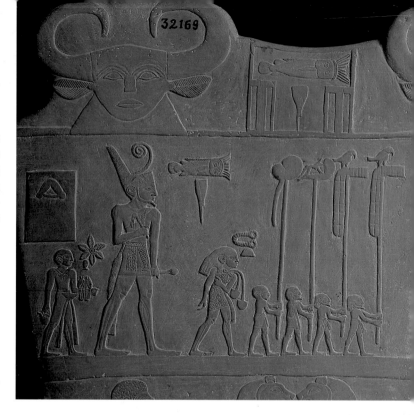

Left: the Bent Pyramid of Dahshur with the lake in the foreground.

Top right: the reverse side of Narmer's Palette. Here the Pharaoh is wearing the Red Crown of Lower Egypt and is followed by his sandal-bearer. Four priests, smaller in size, stand in front of him carrying fetishes.

Right: the front side of Narmer's Palette. Here the Pharaoh Narmer is smashing the head of his kneeling enemy, probably a citizen of Lower Egypt. Behind the Pharaoh stand his sandal-bearer. Above the enemy is the Pharaoh incarnated as the hawk-god, Horus, holding the enemy with a rope with his strong right hand. The enemy lies within the papyrus marches of the Delta.

Page 20: the magnificent diorite statue of Pharaoh Chephren. This hard stone has been worked with excellent skill. The smoothly polished surface gives a natural appeal to the muscular body. The viewer is left in awe as he stands in front of this spectacular statue, which gives the feeling of looking at a divine ruler. The features of Chephren in the statue are very similar to those of his Sphinx *(page 21)*. In both he wears the *nemes* headdress ornamented with a cobra. The Pharaoh, his face dressed up with a false beared, sits on his throne with a slightly dreamy look in his eyes. In his right hand he once had a flail, the symbol of the wealth coming from the soil of the Nile Valley.

This statue was found at the valley temple of his pyramid, one of 23 statues that once stood there. All were ruined in ancient times; Egyptian Museum.

Chephren, the son of Cheops, came to the throne after the death of his elder brother Pharaoh Djedefre, who ruled only briefly. He returned the royal necropolis to Giza and built a pyramid there next to his father's. He built the valley temple with granite, and also carved the biggest and most famous sculpture of all times—the Great Sphinx. This is 72m long, and has Chephren's head and the body of a recumbent lion.

Origin of the Pyramids

The Old Kingdom reached the zenith of its building achievement in the Fourth Dynasty, with the Great Pyramid of Cheops rising above all the others.

Khufu, or Cheops as the Greeks named him, was the son of the Pharaoh Snefru. He built the greatest architectural achievement in the world. The Great Pyramid of Khufu was built with incredible accuracy in terms of cardinal alignment, geometrical shape and proportions and level to within a few mm. It is the largest pyramid in Egypt and was the tallest man-made structure in the world until 1888. Inside the Great Pyramid the Grand Gallery is surely the work of genius. The pyramid is so large that it is almost impossible to fully grasp it in one view.

To understand the significance of Cheops's pyramid one must know something about its predecessors; this section will therefore be devoted to examining the origin of the pyramid and to showing how it may have developed from earlier forms. Scholars reached the conclusion that development of pyramid shape is not only the result of architectural experiments or experiments regarding structural equilibrium. The development is mainly stimulated religiously and politically.

Because the sun sets in the west, the Ancient Egyptians believed that the west was the domain of the dead, whom they defined as the 'Westerners'. In the west the sun-god's boat, having crossed the sky by day, entered its nightly journey through the Underworld or Netherworld. Therefore, all burials were erected on the west bank of the Nile, on the edge of the Western Desert. The east bank of the Nile was the home of the living.

But what was the purpose of these buildings? The answer is quite simple; they were the tombs of the Pharaohs. All of them, from the largest to the smallest, contain, or have contained, sar-

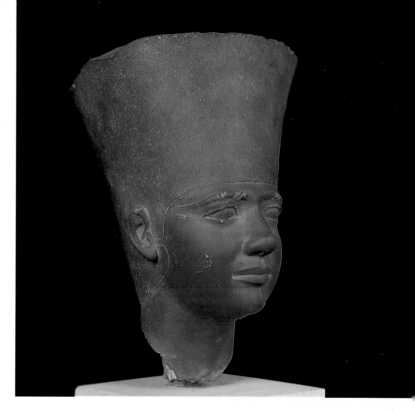

Left and top right: head of Pharaoh Userkaf (45 cm), founder of the Fifth Dynasty, sculpted in schist. The eyebrows are elongated. The statue was found at the sun temple at Abusir in 1957. Userkaf reigned from 2498 to 2491 BC. Here the Pharaoh is wearing the Red Crown of Lower Egypt. It is very rare for Old Kingdom sculpture to represent a Pharaoh wearing the crown of Lower Egypt; Cairo Museum.

Userkaf became Pharaoh by marrying the half-sister of his predecessor Shepseskaf, who might not have had any sons to inherit the throne. Userkaf had no royal blood and nothing is known about his background. His reign was short because he did not come to the throne as a young man.

Right: the ruins of Userkaf's pyramid at Sakkara. The pyramid was damaged in antiquity. The funerary temple was located south of the pyramid. In its courtyard stood a colossal statue of Userkaf. Only the head escaped damage and is now in Cairo Museum.

cophagi, and most bear the names of the Pharaohs whose tombs they were. Some people, awed by the Great Pyramid of Cheops, have rejected this explanation as being dull. They have arranged elaborate theories seeking to prove that Cheops's pyramid was an astronomical observatory measurement site, the dimensions of which are a model of our earth and solar system. Furthermore, they have interpreted its dimensions as a chronological guide to the principal events of past and future history. These beliefs were more prevalent in the 19th century, until Sir Flinders Petrie scientifically demolished them in his great work *The Pyramids and Temples of Gizeh*. Today, though the theories still have their followers, we believe that most people will find more wonder in the archaeologist's vision of how this mighty pyramid was planned and built in an age which possessed no more elaborate mechanical tools than the lever, the roller and the inclined plane.

The Pharaohs of the First and Second Dynasties were buried in brick- or stone-built pits divided into chambers and covered by rectangular structures of sun-dried brick, also divided into compartments containing food, weapons, furniture, and other objects needed in the afterlife. These structures are known as "mastabas", an Arabic word meaning bench. They are so called because when buried in drift sand, the upper projecting portion looks like the stone benches outside farmers' houses. Thousands have been excavated, and some of the finest of the archaic mastabas have been found by Emery at Sakkara. One found in 1937 was 41 metres long and 16 metres wide; it covered five subterranean chambers originally roofed with wooden beams and planks. The clay seals of food and wine jars found in this tomb bear the name of Aha, whom some Egyptologist identify with Menes, the first Pharaoh of the First Dynasty. During the Third and Fourth Dynasties, when large numbers of mastabas were built for the nobles, the general structure underwent a considerable change. The body was buried in a small subterranean chamber at the foot of a deep shaft hewn out of the rock. The mud-brick superstructure, instead of being hollowed into numerous rooms, became almost solid, except for a small offering chamber on the west side. In time mud-brick gave place to stone, until later mastabas became a solid mass of masonry, set apart from the offering-chamber, where relatives and friends of the dead man could place food for the sustenance of his *ba* or

The statue of the seated scribe. He has a scroll of papyrus on his lap, and is ready to write with his right hand. But the pen has disappeared. His hair is black, head and neck are orange-brown coloured, the rest of the body lighter coloured with less orange tan. An unfinished band around the neck represents a necklace. He has inlaid eyes, fringed with copper representing eye-paint. The lower part of the body and legs are a little rough. The statue was found in Sakkara, *c.* 2470 BC, Cairo Museum.

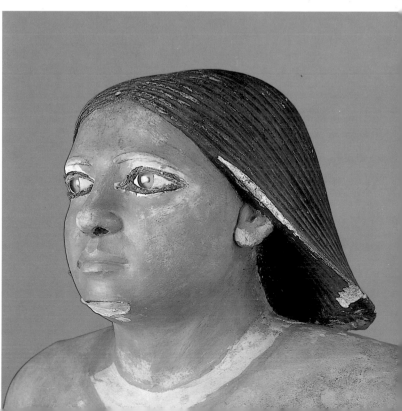

spirit. The *ba* was the spiritual element in man that separated from his physical element after death, but was still dependent on the presence of the earthly body, which had therefore to be preserved.

Burying the body at the foot of a deep rock-cut shaft solved some problems, but created others. The body was now much safer from attack by robbers but it was also further away from the offering chamber. How could the relatives of the dead man be sure that the spirit would receive the food they brought for it? The Ancient Egyptians overcame the problem in a practical way. Into the masonry of the mastaba, they built a chamber to contain a life-size statue of the deceased that represented him exactly as he appeared in life. These beautiful statues were never intended to be seen by the living. They were put in a dark chamber called a *serdab* in Arabic, meaning cellar. Only a narrow opening at the eye-level of the statue enabled it to 'see' into the offering chamber beyond. The spirit of the dead man, recognising his likeness in this statue, could then inhabit it and accept the offerings. Most of the masterpieces of Old Kingdom sculpture which adorn the museums of the world came from mastaba tombs. They are magnificent works of art.

Left and top right: wooden bust of a male (69 cm), from the Fifth Dynasty, found at Sakkara in 1860. The body and the face are of a young man. Eyes are inlaid. The lower portion has been completely destroyed. The statue was discovered very close to the place where the statue of Sheikh al-Balad *(right)* or Ka-aper was found. Some scholars suggested that these statues are of the same man, one when he was young the other when he was old.

Right: wooden statue of Ka-aper (112 cm) or Sheikh al-Balad. The Arabic name Sheikh al-Balad means the 'elder of a village'. However, Ka-aper was a priest during the Fifth Dynasty. This statue is one of the most magnificent non-royal statues of the Old Kingdom. Standing in front of this statue the viewer is left in awe. It realises the Ancient Egyptian definition of eternity. It seems so real that one thinks that the priest is standing live in front of us, and that he will live forever. For Old Kingdom statues this figure has an unusual pose. The body weight is partly on the left leg and partly on the stick that he is holding in his left arm. The left leg is advanced while he was about to lift or move his rear leg. His head is rounded and bold. His figure is somewhat chubby. The eyes are inlaid with crystal and fringed with copper; the arms are separately made and fixed to the body. His kilt is long and knotted at his belly. The stick that he holds is new. The statue was found at Sakkara in 1860; Cairo Museum.

The drawing is from *Egypt, Descriptive, Historical and Picturesque* by Professor Georg Ebers, Leipzig, 1879.

The Step Pyramid of Djoser

The most ancient pyramid surviving in Egypt was built by the Pharaoh Djoser (2668 - 2649 BC), founder of the Third Dynasty, at Sakkara. This is the famous Step Pyramid, so called because it is built in a series of terraces. In fact, it is the oldest large stone building in the world. Here, one witnesses the beginning of architecture, the first attempt by man to build monumentally in stone. Even today after generations of looters have stripped its fine limestone casing, Djoser's great monument is still a source of fascination; not only for the pyramid itself, but also for the marvellous buildings which surround it.

To appreciate its full significance, one should remember that even as late as the end of the Second Dynasty, Pharaoh Khasekhemui, Djoser's predecessor, built his mastaba of sun dried brick, using stone only to line the burial-chamber. Djoser himself built at Beit Khallaf, near Abydos, a massive brick mastaba which he seems never to have used. Then, apparently without precedent, arises this enormous structure of stone, surrounded by an elaborate complex of stone buildings exhibiting amazing artistic design and craftsmanship. The genius who planed this work was the Pharaoh's chief architect, Imhotep, who was adored by later generations of Egyptians as a traditional wise man. He was also regarded as a philosopher and magician.

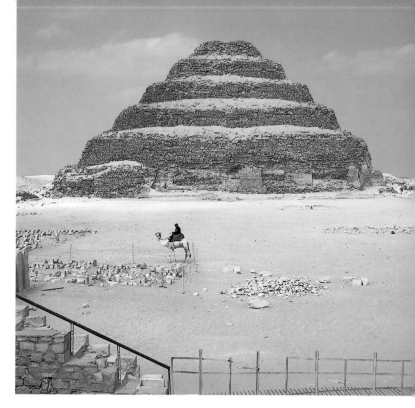

Left and top right: the southern face of Djoser's Step Pyramid.

The Step Pyramid is regarded as the first large stone building raised on earth. The genius who constructed this monument was Imhotep, whose titles are inscribed at the base of a broken statue of Djoser. It says "The treasurer of the Pharaoh of Lower Egypt, the first after the Pharaoh of Upper Egypt, Administrator of the Great Palace, Hereditary Lord, the High Priest of Heliopolis, Imhotep, the builder ..." Imhotep had a legendary reputation not only because of his architectural achievements but also because of his wisdom. In the New Kingdom he was described as a 'patron of scribes', and became the local god of Memphis. He was considered an intermediary on behalf of men who had difficulties. The Greeks knew him as Imhoues and equated him with their god of medicine, Askleopios.

The Step Pyramid began as a *mastaba*, and was later expanded by building on top of it six unequal mastabas, rising to a height of 62 m. Below the pyramid is a vast network of tunnels and shafts. Many were dug by illegal diggers and thieves. A large number of vases was found in the tunnels. Also found was a mummified left leg, which might be the only thing the robbers left behind of Pharaoh Djoser. A mummy of a young boy was also found in an alabaster coffin.

Right: the burial chamber's entrance, made of Aswan granite. It lies below ground level and is approached by a sloping corridor from the north.

To the Egyptologist, the most significant fact concerning the Step Pyramid is that it began not as a pyramid, but as a simple stone mastaba. A close study of the structure reveals that there were five distinct stages in its development before it acquired its present form. First the Pharaoh Djoser built a mastaba like the one at Khallaf, but it was square instead of rectangular and made out of stone, not brick. As his reign continued, he extended it on all four sides, but the exterior was about two feet less in length than the original structure so that a step was formed. He altered it again, making it oblong. Still unsatisfied, he adopted a new plan. He enlarged the mastaba a fourth time and superimposed on top of it a series of three mastabas, each smaller than the one below, thus forming a step pyramid. This seems to have appealed to him, so he extended the base still further until it measured 123 x 107 metres. On this, he built his final Step Pyramid with six terraces and covered the pyramid with fine Tura limestone casing. What we see today is the Step Pyramid without the limestone casing.

The Step Pyramid was surrounded by a series of buildings and a massive wall with a perimeter of over two kilometres and a height of more than 10 metres. Apart from a mortuary temple and a *serdab* containing the statue of the dead Pharaoh, these buildings are in duplicate and simulate small buildings used in ceremonies during the Pharaoh's life.

At the time of its completion, the Step Pyramid must have been the wonder of its age, and it remained so for many subsequent generations in Ancient Egypt. No building like this had ever been raised on earth before. It had within its chambers wall panels decorated in blue glazed tiles; large statues of the Pharaoh in seated and standing poses; stelae in delicate relief representing the athletic figure of Djoser performing rituals explained in hieroglyphic inscriptions; the coffin of an infant made out of plywood and tens of thousands of alabaster and breccia vessels. All these treasures were in addition to those that have been stolen in ancient times.

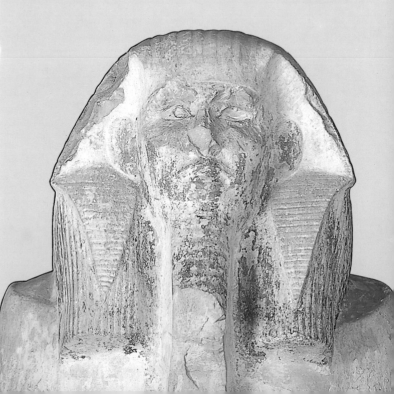

Left and right: one of the first life-size statues of a Pharaoh. The limestone statue of Pharaoh Djoser was found in a *serdab* next to his Step Pyramid of Sakkara. He is represented seated, wearing the garment of the jubilee festival. His royal head cover extends to his neck but does not conceal his ears. Originally the statue was covered with plaster and was painted. The inscription on the base reads the royal Horus name Netjery-khet. The crystal eyes were taken away by robbers, Cairo Museum.

The Turin Papyrus states that Djoser reigned for 19 years and was titled 'Pharaoh of Upper and Lower Egypt'.

Top right: the western face of the Step Pyramid.

The Successors of Djoser

The architectural style of the Step Pyramid was used by Djoser's immediate successors who, however, were unable to complete the buildings. The complex of Pharaoh Sekhem-khet, south-west of the Step Pyramid, has more massive forms of building, using huge stone blocks with no sign of mud-brick. The Pharaoh reigned for about six years, but his temples were also unfinished. The unfinished base is a square measuring 130 metres in length, and the total height is about seven metres. The entrance of the pyramid lies in the northern face. When the builders suddenly stopped working they left the ramp, which practically covered the monument, and it was found *in situ*. As the stages of the pyramid rose, the construction ramps would have risen with it. The building stones came through the ramp. When the Antiquities Department uncovered the entrance in 1954, they were under the impression that no one had entered the pyramid in modern times, because the blocking stone at the entrance was intact. In the subterranean passage leading to the chambers below the pyramid, the excavators of the Antiquities Department found stone and pottery pots and jewellery, as well as mud inscriptions of the unknown Pharaoh Sekhem-khet. The jewellery included 21 gold bracelets of various sizes, a pair of electrum tweezers, a gold necklace and a small gold box. In another chamber, the alabaster sarcophagus was found empty. Archaeologists believe that this was an honorary tomb. However, the remains of a wooden stick, found on top of the sarcophagus, suggest that this had been used by the ancient robbers to remove its lid.

Left: wooden bust of a woman (61 cm). The bust is all that is left of the life-size statue. She wears a headdress that covers her ears. This statue was also found at Sakkara in 1860, very close to Ka-aper, leading some archaeologists to believe she could be his wife; Cairo Museum.

Top right: drawing of a seated scribe now in the Louvre from *Egypt, Descriptive, Historical and Picturesque* by Professor Georg Ebers, Leipzig, 1879.

Right: the remains of Pharaoh Unas's pyramid, Sakkara. Unas was the last Pharaoh of the Fifth Dynasty. The pyramid's height measured 43 m, its base 57.5 m. All the limestone casing was removed in antiquity except for a small part on its southern side. Also completely destroyed is the funerary temple on its eastern side. The entrance is, as usual, from the northern side. The two inner rooms have inclined roofs decorated with astronomical figures. The walls are covered with hieroglyphs of a text is known as the 'Pyramid Texts', a religious text praising the soul of the deceased Pharaoh to triumph over hostile power before it is united with the divine Ra.

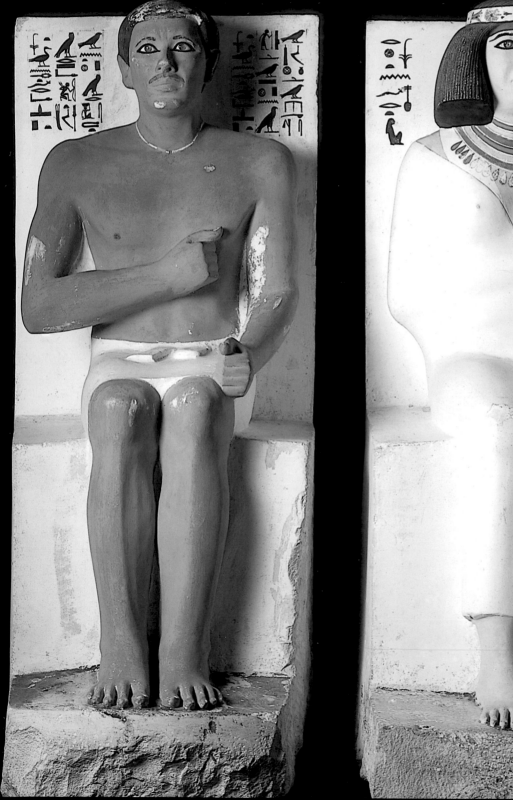

Snefru, a Legendary and Beloved Pharaoh

The Pharaoh Snefru, founder of the Fourth Dynasty, came to the throne by marrying Queen Hetepheres, daughter of Pharaoh Huni. Snefru's mother was a member of the Pharaoh Huni's harem. By marrying Huni's daughter, who was also his half-sister, Snefru confirmed by blood legitimacy his right to the throne. He was a legendary figure, and his reign seems to have been glorious. The Palermo Stone, a valuable source of information on the Pharaohs of the Old Kingdom, mentions that he sent a fleet of 40 vessels to Lebanon to get cedar wood. Many of these wooden beams, still in good condition, are inside the Bent Pyramid in Dahshur. The Palermo Stone also mentions that he crushed a revolt in Nubia and captured 7,000 prisoners. Control of Nubia was crucial in guarding the trade routes for African goods such as ebony, incense, panther skins, etc. It also allowed Egypt to dominate the gold mines of the Nubian desert. Inscriptions of Snefru were found in the mines of Wadi Maghara in Sinai. His campaigns in Sinai were not aimed at nomads or invaders from Sinai and Palestine; his goal was to use the copper, turquoise and malachite mines in the western region of Sinai at Wadi Nasb and Wadi Maghara. He was considered a kind and beloved Pharaoh. In fact, the cult of Snefru flourished for centuries after his death.

Snefru is the only Pharaoh in Egypt who has four pyramids attributed to him. He completed the pyramid at Meidum, which had been started by his predecessor Pharaoh Huni. Then he abandoned the Meidum Pyramid. Some archaeologists speculate that his con-

Left and right: pair statue of prince Ra-Hotep, the high priest of Heliopolis and commander of the army, and his wife Nofert. The two figures are represented seated on a square cut chair. Ra-Hotep has his right arm folded on his chest and his left arm on his knees. The statues are painted, the eyes are inlaid with crystal and outlined with black. Nofert wears a necklace, and surmounting her head is a heavy black wig that reaches her shoulders. On her forehead is a band ornamented with a floral design. Her eyes are smaller than those of Ra-Hotep. The skin colour of the man is reddish-brown, while the woman's is creamy yellow. It is customary in Egyptian art to represent men as darker than women. This pair statue, found in a tomb near the Pyramid of Meidum, is regarded as one of the magnificent statues of the Old Kingdom, *c.* 2600 BC, Cairo Museum.

Top right: the mortuary temple of the Meidum Pyramid, the oldest mortuary temple so far discovered.

A graffito from a much later era, the 18th dynasty, identifies the temple of the pyramid as being the temple of Pharaoh Snefru. This implies that the temple was still in good condition as late as the 18th dynasty and that the Egyptians of the New Kingdom believed this pyramid had belonged to Snefru.

tribution to transfer the so far step pyramid into a true pyramid was unstable and the outer casing began to collapse. He then chose Dahshur, a new site closer to Memphis, to build his gigantic tomb. At Dahshur he built the Bent Pyramid and the Northern or Red Pyramid. The choice of Meidum must have been an intentional attempt to breach with some religious cults. His family may have had some links with the Fayoum region. Nefermaat, who was Pharaoh Huni's architect and Snefru's vizier, is buried in Fayoum. Nefermaat's son Hemiunu was Cheops's architect and was responsible for building the Great Pyramid. Hemiunu's tomb, which contains a statue of him, is in Giza. Snefru also built a fourth pyramid at Seila in Fayoum; this pyramid has no burial chamber and its remains are only seven metres high. The pyramid has been known for more than a hundred years, but its owner was identified only in the 1980s.

Ahmed Fakhry thinks that Snefru's contribution to the Meidum Pyramid was the last phase in the construction, described by Ludwig Borchardt as transforming an eight-stepped pyramid into a true pyramid with smooth casing stone.

The Westcar Papyrus. The Westcar Papyrus, now in the Berlin Museum, dates from the Hyksos Period. It mentions Snefru as a courageous Pharaoh, but shows he also had a worldly side. The papyrus tells a story quoted to Prince Bauefre, a son of Cheops. The story is that one day Snefru was bored in his palace. His priest suggested that the Pharaoh to be taken out to the lake, and rowed by some of the beautiful ladies of the palace. Snefru liked the idea and ordered, "Let there brought to me twenty nets, and let these nets be given to these women when they have taken off their clothes ... and the heart of His Majesty was happy at this sight of their rowing." However the trip came to a sudden stop when one of the ladies lost a turquoise charm from her tresses and refused to continue. The Pharaoh offered to replace her lost piece, but she insisted on retrieving it. So the Pharaoh again consulted the priest, but in this respect as a magician. He immediately caused the water to part and found the missing object on the bottom. Then the rowing continued.

Left: portrait of Princess Nofert. The diadem on her forehead has a beautiful floral design, showing how the Ancient Egyptians loved nature.

Top right: the northern face of the Meidum Pyramid showing the modern steps leading to the original entrance.

Right: the southern face of the Meidum pyramid. This pyramid has a tower-like structure. The original casing is well preserved.

The Meidum Pyramid

The Meidum Pyramid, although a *true* pyramid, has a construction plan based on the Third Dynasty step pyramids *(see below)*. However, the builders set up new standards that were followed by all subsequent pyramids. These were:

1. Entry on the northern face.

2. Side inclination angle at 51° 53′. All subsequent pyramids have inclination angles between 51° and 54°, the only exception being the Northern Pyramid of Dahshur which has an inclination angle of 43°.

3. Descending passage slopes down at 26°.

4. The burial chamber is supported by a corbelled roof. In line with Third Dynasty traditions the burial chamber axis is from north to south. However, in all subsequent pyramids the burial chamber lies from west to east.

5. The mortuary temple lies on the pyramid's eastern side. Third Dynasty traditions place the mortuary temple on the northern side of the pyramid.

6. A causeway connects the mortuary temple to the valley temple, down the valley.

The Meidum Pyramid was built to a height of 92 metres, with a square base having a side length of 144 metres. Its side inclination angle is 51° 50′ 35″. Petrie found that the pyramid's core was a

Left and right: the Pyramid of Meidum was a transitional stage of development from the step pyramid to the full pyramid. The tower-shaped pyramid was originally built as a step pyramid and later modified into a true pyramid by additional casing. This turned out to be a difficult task, and it collapsed. Several theories have been put forward to explain the reason for the collapse, for example that the pyramid was never finished and the collapse occurred during construction. This theory is based on the fact that the stelae at the temple near the pyramid was not finished and that the rough burial chamber was also left unfinished.

The pyramid is surrounded by debris of its collapsed outer casing. The original entrance lies on the northern face, below the hole cut into the superstructure by ancient thieves.

The pyramid was built by Huni, the last Pharaoh of the Third Dynasty, and completed by Snefru, the first Pharaoh of the Fourth Dynasty. Little of Huni's achievements are known. His name is in the canon of Turin but not on the Abydos list. No inscription of him survived on stone and there are no statues of him.

Top right: the picture is photographed from the top of the Meidum Pyramid. It shows the ancient causeway starting at the valley temple, not yet excavated, and ending at the mortuary temple shown in the picture with the two stelae. These are the oldest valley temple and causeway so far discovered.

mastaba with eight added layers of masonry, which made it an eight-stepped pyramid. Petrie also dug a tunnel that reached the core of the pyramid. Through this tunnel he was able to show that the pyramid was constructed of inclined layers of limestone blocks with a slope of 75°. This arrangement of inclination towards the middle of the pyramid increased the structural stability of the building. All later true pyramids were constructed by horizontal layers of limestone blocks arranged on top of each other. These inclined layers were a common building practice in the Third Dynasty. According to Borchardt, the later layers E1 and E2 were added after the building had been completed. They were also arranged with the inclined type of construction. Layer E3 was added later to transform the so-far step pyramid to a true pyramid. The blocks of E3 were arranged horizontally. This was the first achievement of a *true* pyramid. The casing blocks of E3 have disappeared; they could have been stripped off intentionally as was the fate of almost all pyramids in the Middle Ages. Some scholars have suggested that the whole E3 arrangement was unstable because it was built on the smooth casing stone of the so-far step pyramid. Borchardt thinks that the E3 steps slid during the last phase of construction and must have buried the workers beneath the rubble. What we see today are the E2 layers with their original fine casing limestone.

On the east side of the pyramid Petrie unearthed a small mortuary temple, the first mortuary temple to be built east of the pyramid. So far, in all Third Dynasty pyramids the mortuary temple was built north of the pyramid.

Today the pyramid is surrounded by a heap of debris. It is hoped that removal of this debris will reveal many unknown facts about Fourth-Dynasty architecture. It was in a tomb close to this pyramid that the famous statues of Prince Ra-Hotep and his wife, Princess Nofert, were found by Mariette (see pictures pages 34 - 36).

The entrance, as in all pyramids, lies in the middle of the northern face at an elevation of 16.6 metres above the ground. A 57-metre-long passage descends inside the pyramid reaching a horizontal chamber that leads to an upward shaft, with the burial chamber at the top. The floor of the base chamber lies at the same

Left : the northern face of the Meidum Pyramid. The original limestone casing is well preserved. This is the layer defined as E2 above and in the cross-section on the next page. The hole shown was cut into the superstructure by ancient thieves.
Top right: the eastern face of the Meidum Pyramid.
Right: the southern face of the Meidum Pyramid.

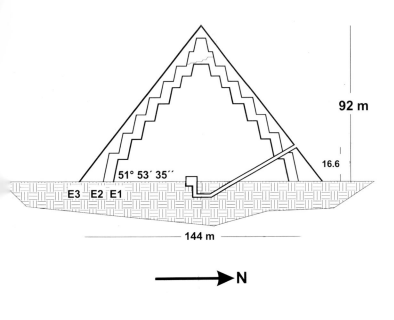

92 m

51° 53′ 35″

16.6

E3 E2 E1

144 m

N

level as the base of the pyramid. In this chamber, Petrie in 1891 found the remains of a wooden coffin which he thought probably belonged to the Pharaoh Snefru. In the roof are holes that were used as sockets for the wooden beams, exactly similar to the cedarwood beams found inside the Bent Pyramid also built by Snefru.

The ruins of a small pyramid lie on the southern side of the Meidum Pyramid. On the east is a small mortuary temple with its own enclosure wall, which was almost intact when discovered by Petrie. On the inside walls are graffiti written by visitors, some of which refer to the Pharaoh Snefru. One of dates from the end of the Old Kingdom, but most are from the XVIIIth Dynasty. An inscription from the year 41 of Tuthmosis III's reign was written by the scribe Aakheperkare-senebe who wrote that he had come here to see the beautiful temple of Snefru. He prayed for the *ka* of Pharaoh Snefru and of Queen Meresankh: "May cool myrrh rain down from the heavens and fragment incense drip onto the temple roof of Horus Snefru." This inscription and other similar texts ascertain that the owner of the Meidum Pyramid was Snefru.

A computer reconstruction of the Meidum Pyramid showing the descending corridor and burial chamber. The blue 'hyper-plane' demonstrates that the descending passage and burial chamber lie in the middle of the pyramid exactly below the apex.

Left: the Meidum Pyramid viewed from southeast.

Right: the burial chamber inside the Meidum Pyramid. This was the first construction of a corbelled roof, which has seven steps. It is roughly hewn and lacks the grandiose style of the burial chamber and the two antechambers at the Northern Pyramid of Dahshur.

The 57m-long descending passage reaches two small antechambers. An upward vertical shaft leads to the burial chamber, which measures 5.9 X 2.6 m, with axis from north to south. Its height is five metres. The floor of the burial chamber is at the same level as the base of the pyramid. Gaston Maspero, who was the first to enter the pyramid in modern times (1882), found no sarcophagus.

The Bent Pyramid at Dahshur

Snefru also built the Bent Pyramid and the Northern or Red Pyramid at Dahshur. The Bent Pyramid was planned from the beginning as a true pyramid, with its sides measuring 188.6 metres and with an original height of 101 metres. Its casing stone is the best preserved of all the pyramids of Egypt. The angle of slope is 54° 31′13′′ up to a height of 49 metres, and then it becomes 43° 21′. The change of the sloping angle gives the pyramid the name 'Bent Pyramid'. Archaeologists explain the change of the sloping angle by speculating that it was too steep to continue, and the centre of weight of the core masonry stones would make the structure unstable. Another explanation is that the builders may have felt that the casing stone was unstable and would fall out. However, cracks were discovered in the passage leading to the upper burial chamber. The builders tried to repair the damage by filling it with plaster. This might have been a strong reason for the builders to reduce the pyramid's slope. This modification resulted in reducing the weight of the upper part of the pyramid, thereby reducing the loads on the chambers and passages that had started to crack.

The Bent Pyramid is unique not only in its shape but also in having two separate entrances, one situated roughly in the middle of the northern face about 12 metres above the ground, the other on the west face. This last entry is the only known exception to the rule that all pyramid entrances lay on the north face. The west entrance was opened by Ahmed Fakhry in 1951. Each entrance leads to a separate chamber; the north to a subterranean chamber, the west to a chamber at ground level and a little to the south east above the other. The corridor at the northern entrance has a slope of 25° 24 and is 79 metres long, and leading to a small chamber with a corbelled roof 12,5 metres high. Then immediately follow-

Snefru abandoned the royal necropolis at Meidum and chose the new site of Dahshur. He is the only Pharaoh who built four pyramids. It has been calculated that he used 3.7 million cubic metres of construction material.

The slope of the lower part of the Bent Pyramid is 54° 31′13′′ to a height of 49 metres, and then becomes 43° 21′.

Along the southern face of the Bent Pyramid is a small satellite pyramid *(left)* which still retains some of its original limestone casing at the base. The entrance is still approachable though a passageway that reveals only sand and debris. Inside this pyramid is a prototype or miniature Grand Gallery, that is, a corbelled sloping chamber that leads to the burial chamber. This design innovation demonstrates the evolution of pyramids in the Old Kingdom as this concept would later appear in grander form in the Great Pyramid of Cheops.

Right: the solid construction of the Bent Pyramid and its sharp change of angle are very evident.

ing comes the subterranean chamber, measuring 6.2 metres from north to south and 4.9 metres from east to west with a height of 17.1 metres. Its corbeled roof with 15 courses looks very impressive. At the top, it is only 1.6 metres long and 0.3 metres wide. A narrow passage starting from a height of 12.6 metres on the southern wall reaches the chamber at ground level. This passage is roughly hewn, and it looks as if it was cut later by ancient thieves. Both chambers have a similar wall and ceiling with a corbeled roof. The interesting feature about this second chamber is that it

Left and top right: the Bent Pyramid is unusual in that it has two entrances. The west entrance is the only known exception in the Old Kingdom. All entrances of other pyramids lie on its northern face. Here the entrance lies about 15m south of the centre of the western face. The entrance descends for a length of 63m first with an angle of 30° 9′, and then with an angle of 24° 17′ until it reaches ground level. It then continues horizontally until it leads to the upper chamber.

Top: the valley temple of the Bent Pyramid was discovered by the eminent Egyptologist Ahmed Fakhry.

Right: in front of the pyramid at the centre of its east side lie the remains of the mortuary temple of Snefru. The temple was discovered by Ahmed Fakhry in 1951. He also cleared the causeway and found the valley temple at the edge of the cultivation. Ahmed Fakhry thinks that the mortuary temple was small when built before undergoing several enlargements.

has various cedarwood beams fixed between the walls. They were in a stunning state of preservation when discovered by Perring and Vyse in 1839. These cedar beams must have been part of the cargo that Snefru imported from Lebanon. At first sight one would think the wooden beams were kind of a raised platform for workmen, but the conclusion reached by the explorers and other archaeologists was that this could not have been their function. When Perring and Vyse first entered the pyramid they found some white limestone blocks among the beams. This arrangement of white limestone and wooden beams is still a mystery.

To the south of the Bent Pyramid is a satellite pyramid, probably belonging to Queen Hetepheres I. However, some scholars think that this small pyramid was for the burial of the Pharaoh's viscera or for his *ka*. The interesting feature about this pyramid is that its entrance is at ground level, first through a descending passage and then an ascending passage to the burial chamber. The ascending passage has a corbelled roof approximately seven metres high, a miniature version of the 'Grand Gallery' in the Great Pyramid of Cheops. Next to the satellite pyramid south of the Bent Pyramid Fakhry found a large stelae bearing the name of Snefru.

Fakhry thought that quarrymen of the Middle Ages would first dismantle any building close to cultivation before moving on to the pyramid sites further away. He therefore did not expect to find many remains of the valley temple. Contrary to his expectation, however, his workmen unearthed the valley temple and found its walls decorated with excellent reliefs. Up to that day Egyptologists held the common view that valley temples had no reliefs up to the end of the Fourth Dynasty. Fakhry also found on the site statues, three ruins of life-size statues, stelae and many other objects, as well as several reliefs of Snefru. The valley temple measures 47 X 36 m, with its axis directed north-south.

The valley temple of the Bent Pyramid is the oldest valley temple so far discovered. Third Dynasty pyramids had neither valley temples nor causeways. The Meidum Pyramid built by Snefru's predecessor Pharaoh Huni and completed by Snefru had both a causeway and a valley temple, but the valley temple had been totally ruined because it lay below the present water table of the cultivation. It is not known whether the valley temple and causeway were built by Huni or Snefru. It is therefore still not known who introduced this functional transformation to the pyramid complex.

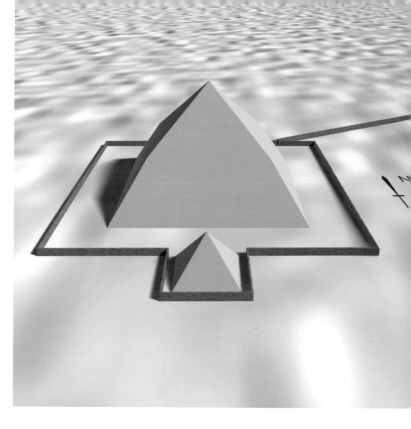

A reconstruction of the Bent Pyramid. This is how the Bent Pyramid looked after it was built in the third millennium BC. The south side contains the smaller subsidiary pyramid which was possibly intended for the Pharoh's wife, Queen Hetepheres.

As a final word about the Bent Pyramid, Ahmed Fakhry said : "The Bent Pyramid has proved to be a hard *talk* for all who have tried to work on it, and it may not yet have revealed all its secrets."

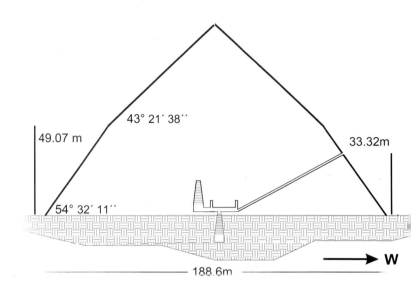

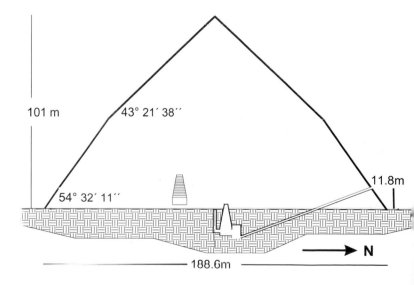

Left: interior of the Bent Pyramid. The green 'hyper-plane' coincides with the west entrance, its descending passage and chamber. It is set off from the centre of the western face by 15m towards the south. The northern entrance, its descending passage and burial chamber coincide with the yellow plane. The dark blue plane is the extension of the yellow plane below ground level.

Left : interior of the Bent Pyramid. The green 'hyper-plane' coincides with the west entrance, its descending passage and chamber. It is set off from the centre of the western face by 15m towards the south. The northern entrance, its descending passage and burial chamber coincide with the orange plane. The brown plane is the extension of the orange plane below ground level.

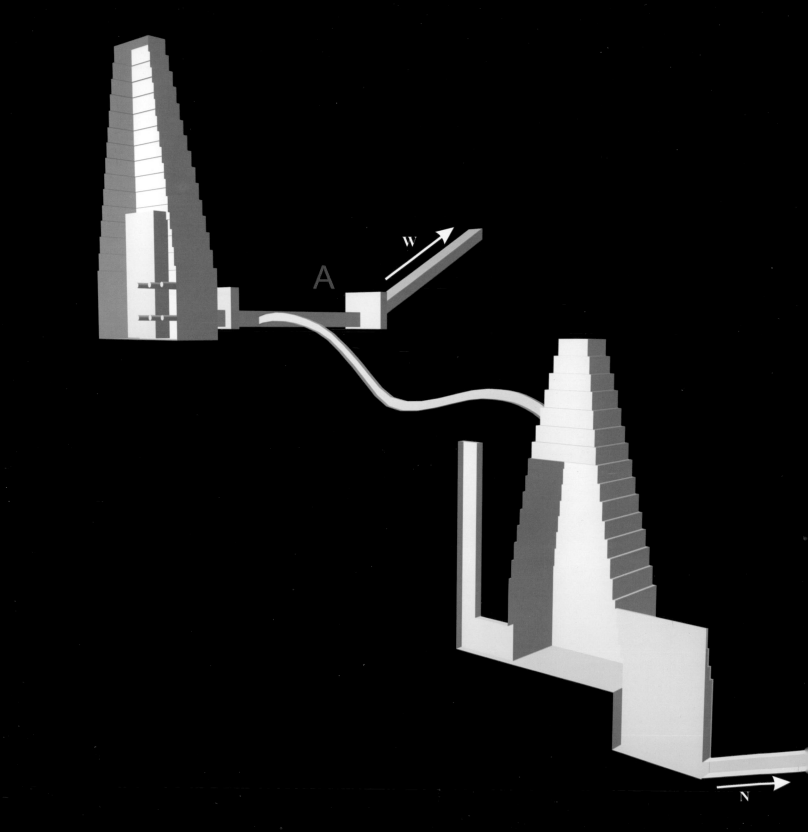

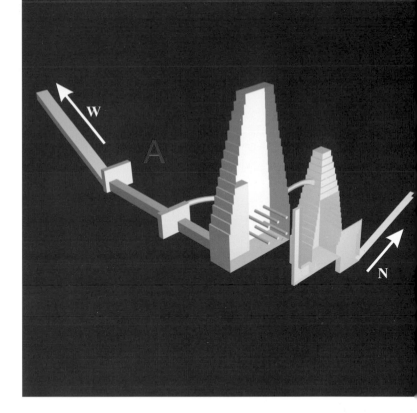

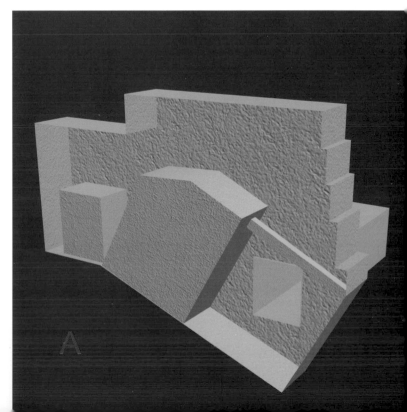

Left and top right: the two interior passages with the upper and lower chambers of the Bent Pyramid.

Right: a section through the centre of the western passage showing the portcullis (A). When the supporting bar is removed the portcullis slides down and closes the passage.

The Northern Pyramid at Dahshur

The oldest true pyramid is the Northern Pyramid at Dahshur, a short distance from the Bent Pyramid. Although earlier in date than the Great Pyramid it is not much smaller in size, the base measuring 220 metres and the height 105 metres. The sides have a slope with the horizontal of 43° 36´, which is nearly equal to the slope of the upper part of the Bent Pyramid (the base of Cheops's pyramid measures 232 metres, and its side has a slope of 51° 51´14.3´´ to the horizontal). The slope is much less than most other pyramids, and gives it more or less a flattened appearance.

The entrance of the pyramid through the northern face is 28 metres above the ground, and descends with an angle of 27° 56´ (the angle of descent of the sloping passage in Cheops's pyramid is 26° 18´ 9.7´´). The corridor, 60 metres long, leads to three chambers. All these have corbel-vaulted roofs. The first two antechambers are nearly identical in size and form. Each antechamber measures 10 metres in length from north to south, 3.6 metres in width, and 12 metres in height. The second antechamber lies exactly below the apex of the pyramid. An opening eight metres high in the southern wall of the second antechamber leads to the burial chamber, which has a length is nine metres from west to east and a width of 4.2 metres. Its corbelled roof has a height of 15 metres. The floor of the chamber was removed in antiquity to a depth of four metres. The walls were blackened by fire and the torches of ancient thieves and visitors. This is the first burial chamber to be aligned from west to east. In all Third Dynasty pyramids and also the previous two pyramids of Snefru, the burial chambers were aligned from north to south.

The pyramid has no inscriptions, and it was a mystery to find out which Pharaoh was its builder. Several small clues made archaeologists come to the conclusion that its builder was Snefru. Snefru's name was also found written on a casing block at the

Left: the Northern Pyramid at Dahshur is the first true pyramid, with its slopes rising at a gentle angle of 43° 36´ instead of 52°. This became the standard angle of later pyramid's face inclination.

Top right: the first row of limestone casing on the eastern face. Probably this row escaped plundering because it was buried under moving sand and debris.

Right: the capstone or pyramidion that has been recently recovered. This, found broken and reconstructed, was the first capstone of a major pyramid in Egypt to be found. However, the slope of its sides disagrees with that of the pyramid. Archaeologists think that the pyramidion may have been built for the Bent Pyramid before the slope of its sides was changed. It became useless after the slope was changed to 43° 36´and the Northern Pyramid was built with the same slope.

north-eastern corner of the pyramid. However, inscriptions of this order are sometimes inaccurate. In 1905 Ludwig Borchardt saw another such inscription at the edge of the cultivation dating from the reign of Pepi I of the Sixth Dynasty. It was a decree from Pepi I exempting the priests of the 'two pyramids of Snefru' from some taxes.

No sarcophagi or remains of a mummy were found in any of Snefru's pyramids.

Approximately 400 metres east of the pyramid are the remains of a vast Fourth Dynasty necropolis. This has been excavated by Dr. Rainer Stadelmann, head of the German Archaeological Institute. He also excavated the ruins of the Northern Pyramid's mortuary temple, which was not completed at the time of Snefru's death.

At the close of this section on Snefru's pyramids I am sure the reader will raise the question: "In which of the three pyramids was Snefru buried?" Many archaeologists share with Ahmed Fakhry the opinion that Snefru was buried in the upper chamber of the western gallery of the Bent Pyramid. However, Stadelmann thinks that Snefru was buried in the Northern Pyramid, in spite of the fact that the complex was not finished at the time of his death. It is hoped that further research with modern scientific tools will reveal many surprises.

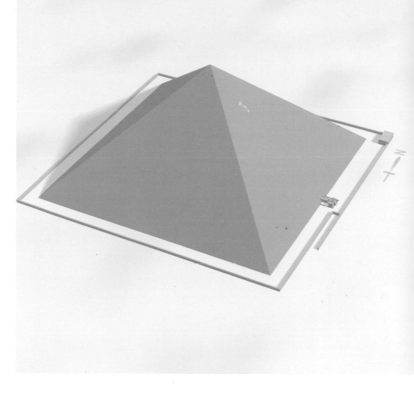

A computer reconstruction of the Northern Pyramid and a photographic image from the northeast.

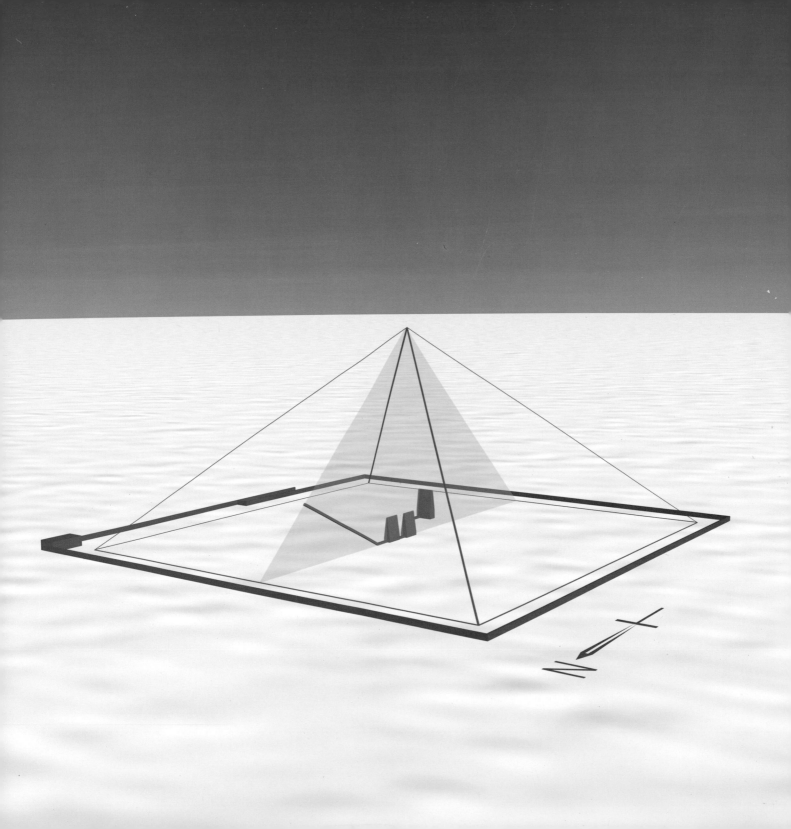

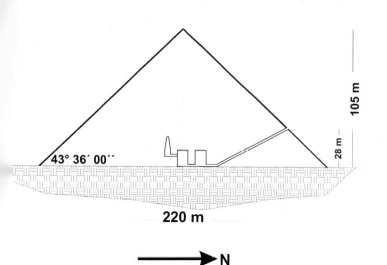

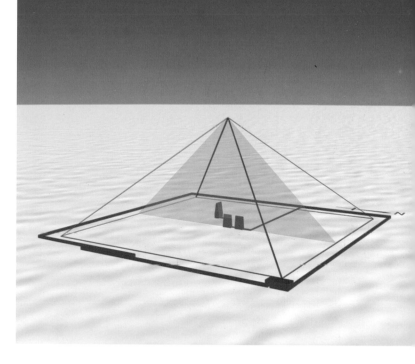

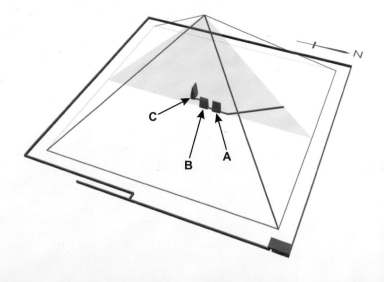

Inside the Northern Pyramid. The orange *(left and top right)* and yellow *(right)* 'hyper-plane' coincides with the entrance, the descending passage and the two antechambers (A, B) and the burial chamber (C).

Right: a modern staircase has been installed to ease the ascent to the opening which is 30m above ground level and four metres east of centre. The 60m-long descending passage *(right)* has a slope of 27º 56′ and is furnished with modern hand rails to help the visitor in the descent. Shown right is the modern ventilation pipe that sucks the air from the burial chamber to control the humidity left by visitors. The end of the descending passageway empties into a level corridor that is approximately eight metres long. This corridor leads to the first antechamber *(left and top right)* (**A** *page 63*) and has a magnificent corbelled roof built in 11 steps and reaching a height of 12 m. The pictures *left and top* are looking south. In the picture *(left)* the camera is held towards the ceiling of the corbelled roof. At the south end of the first antechamber is a small corridor *(top)* which leads to the second antechamber **B**.

The second antechamber (**B** *page 63*) has similar dimensions to that of the first **A**. This chamber lies directly beneath the apex of the pyramids and is exceptional in that it is one of the only pyramid chambers to lie directly beneath the centre-point or apex of the pyramid. At the south end, a modern wooden staircase *(right)* has been installed to allow access to the burial chamber **C,** the entrance for which is located approximately eight metres above the floor of this second chamber. Pictures *(left and top)* are photographed looking north from the wooden staircase of the second chamber **B**. The downward continuation of the *(top)* picture is the *(left)* picture. The top of the stairs leads to a final corridor which is about seven metres long and ends at the burial chamber **C**. The *(top right)* picture is photographed looking towards the corbelled roof.

The burial chamber *(C page 63)* with dimensions of approximately 4.2 X 9 metres with axis from west to east. Its corbelled roof reaches a height of 15 m. Picture *(left and top right)* were photographed looking west. The continuation downward of the *(left)* picture is the *(top right)* picture. In the picture *(top)* the camera is held towards the ceiling to show the corbelled roof. The chamber's floors were removed in antiquity to a depth of four metres in search of hidden chambers and passages. You can see several layers of the pyramid's core masonry *(top right)*. The *(right)* picture is the entrance of the burial chamber **C** from the second antechamber **B**.

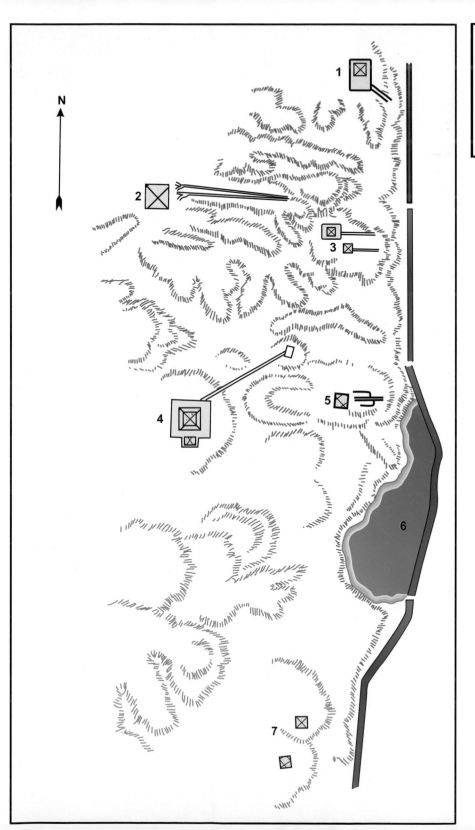

1. Pyramid of Senusert III
2. Northern Pyramid of Snefru
3. Pyramid of Amenemhat II
4. Bent Pyramid of Snefru
5. Pyramid of Amenemhat III
6. Lake of Dahshur
7. Pyramid of Mazghuna

Why the Pyramid Shape?

The above is a short historical description of the evolution of a tomb from a burial pit to a true pyramid. At this point we would like to raise the question: why did the Old Kingdom Pharaohs adopt a pyramid shape for their tombs? Until the first half of the 20th century Egyptologists accepted the theory advanced by the great German archaeologist Ludwig Borchardt, that the shape evolved through a logical process of development from earlier, simpler types of tombs. Discoveries at Sakkara at about the middle of the 20th century, however, have thrown doubt on this explanation, and another theory has been suggested by I. E. S. Edwards, to whom I am indebted for much of the material of this section. Edwards's theory, is fully explained in his book *The Pyramids of Egypt.*

Edwards suggests that the reason for choosing the pyramid shape may have been religious rather than practical. His theory might be summarised as follows: the mastaba tombs of the First and Second-Dynasty Pharaohs were conceived as eternal homes for their owners. The afterlife was to be lived in and around the tomb. Then, at an undetermined period, possibly between the Second and Third Dynasties, a different conception gained ground, that of an afterlife lived with the sun-god. The Pyramid Texts, the earliest religious document known in Egypt, contain a text which states: "A staircase of heaven is laid for him so that he may climb to heaven thereby." It is tempting to believe that the Step Pyramid represented this heavenly staircase. Djoser, as we have seen, built a tomb of each type, a mastaba at Bet Khallaf and a Step Pyramid at Sakkara; there was also a second mastaba in the enclosure wall of the Step Pyramid.

Henry Breasted stated that the true pyramid was nothing more than a large-scale reproduction of the sacred symbol of the sun-god which was kept in the "holy of holies" at Heliopolis. This symbol was a pyramidion, or a miniature pyramid, called the ben-ben. "Why", asks Edwards, "was it chosen?" By way of answer he describes the appearance of the sun's rays as they shine down through a gap of clouds. Was the purpose of the true pyramid to be a material representation of the sun's rays? Edwards also cites evidence to support this theory.

Top right: the remains of Amenemhat III's pyramid, XIIth Dynasty.
Right: the remains of the valley temple of the Bent Pyramid, showing the Bent Pyramid in the background and the remains of the causeway.

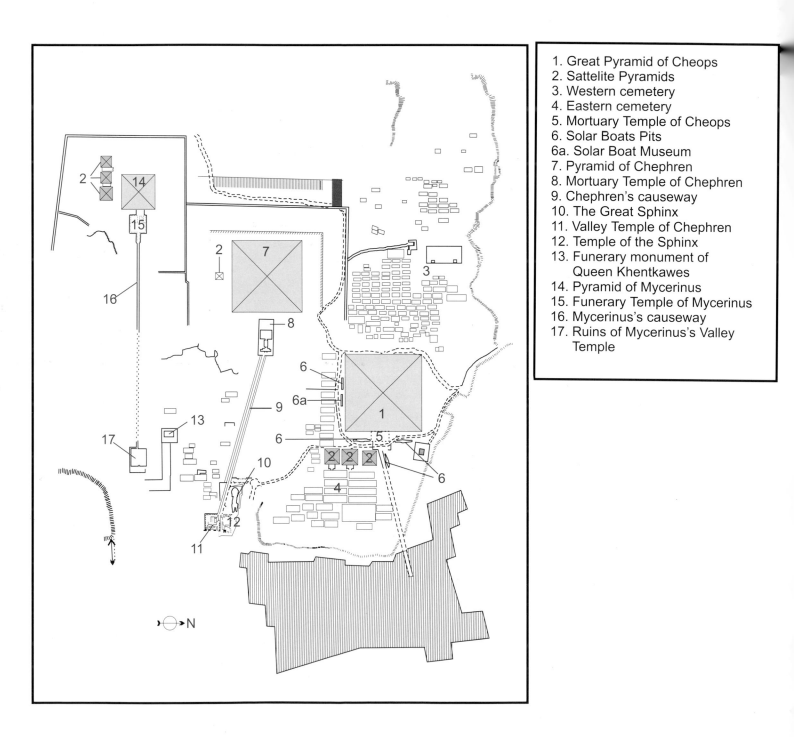

1. Great Pyramid of Cheops
2. Sattelite Pyramids
3. Western cemetery
4. Eastern cemetery
5. Mortuary Temple of Cheops
6. Solar Boats Pits
6a. Solar Boat Museum
7. Pyramid of Chephren
8. Mortuary Temple of Chephren
9. Chephren's causeway
10. The Great Sphinx
11. Valley Temple of Chephren
12. Temple of the Sphinx
13. Funerary monument of
    Queen Khentkawes
14. Pyramid of Mycerinus
15. Funerary Temple of Mycerinus
16. Mycerinus's causeway
17. Ruins of Mycerinus's Valley
    Temple

N

The Great Pyramid of Cheops, Khufu's Horizon

The Great Pyramid is the oldest of the Seven Wonders of the ancient world. It still stands defying time. In fact, it was built to outlive all of humanity. The Great Pyramid is a perfect building and yet so enormous that its construction would exhaust the skills and resources of today's technology almost to breaking point. Yet it is astonishing, and one can find no explanation for the fact that only a hundred years separate this giant building from the construction of Pharaoh Djoser's Step Pyramid at Sakkara, the first large stone building ever raised on earth. And only a couple of centuries separate the Great Pyramid's age from the edge of pre-history.

The Great Pyramid is the most gigantic piece of architecture in the world. The original height of the pyramid was 146 metres, and the volume of the structure is such that it has been calculated that St Peter's in Rome, St Paul's in London, Westminster Abbey and the cathedrals of Florence and Milan could find room within it, were it not solid (see I.E.S. Edwards *The Pyramids of Egypt*). About 2.3 million blocks of stone, weighing on average 2.5 tons a piece, were used to erect this gigantic structure. The stone was quarried from the hills in the east bank of the Nile. When complete, the pyramid was covered from top to bottom with a smooth polished casing of fine limestone and capped by an apex or a pyramidion that reflected the first rays of the sun. On the Great Pyramid only a few casing stones remain at the base of each face. The rest has been stripped off, so that instead of a smooth, shiny surface we see a series of steps. Unfortunately, we do not see the pyramid as it was built or even as Herodotus saw it about 500 BC. The present height of the Great Pyramid is 137 metres. The top capstone is missing. Originally, the length of the sides at ground level was 230.35 metres, but as the Tura sandstone facing has practically all disappeared it is now reduced. The sloping sides were about 187 metres and are now 174 metres. The sides incline at an angle of 51° 51′.

Originally, each of the three pyramids was joined to the Nile by a causeway which served two purposes: first as a road along which quarried stone could be dragged to the pyramid's plateau, and second as a ceremonial way along which the funeral and subsequent procession could pass. At the foot of each causeway near the river was a valley building where certain rituals were performed,

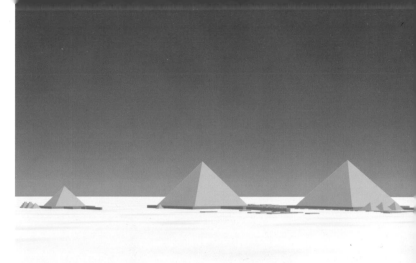

Top right: elevation of the Giza Plateau, looking 135° north east with the sun from the east.

Right: elevation at 315° north east with the sun from the east.

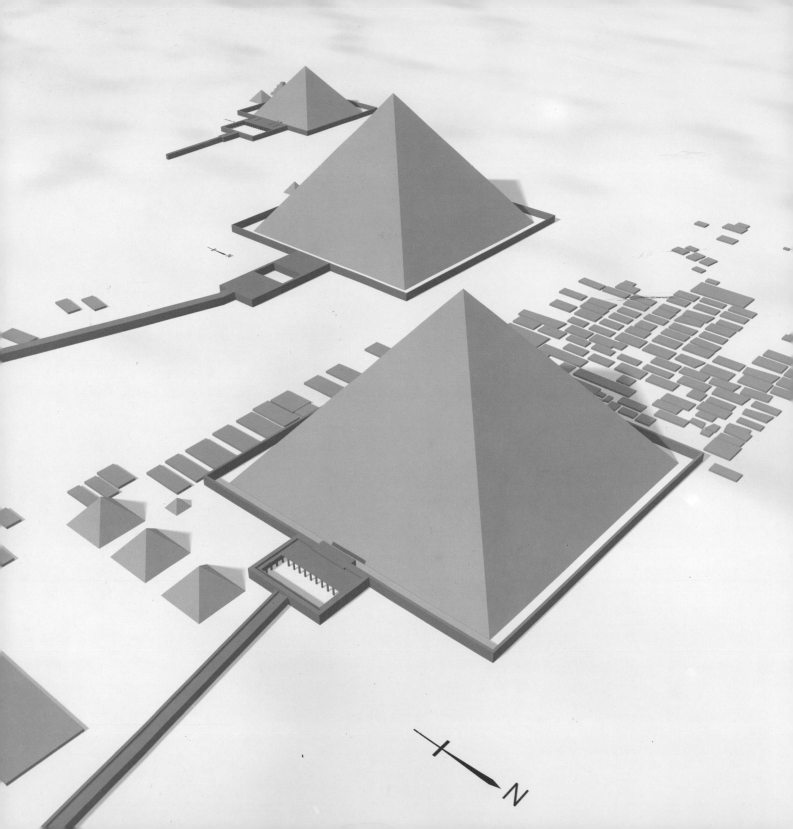

and at the top, under the shadow of the pyramid itself, was a mortuary temple. In the finished state each causeway was roofed, so that it presented a long semi-enclosed corridor. Today nothing remains of the causeways, and apart from the valley building little remains of the temples. But in the days of the Old Kingdom these buildings were an essential part of the pyramid complex. To consider the pyramids in isolation, as they are today, is to get quite a false idea of their original appearance.

The Great Pyramid in Antiquity

Throughout the Middle Kingdom, scant attention was paid to the Great Pyramid. The necropolis was used as a quarry for other temples and buildings. This disregard continued in the New Kingdom, although Prince Khaemwese, the eldest son of Ramses II, worked enthusiastically to renovate the Sakkara and Giza necropolises. In the XXVIth Dynasty a 'renaissance' of old traditions was suddenly awakened throughout the country. People suddenly cared for Old and Middle Kingdom monuments. Nothing in particular is known of what effect this had on the Great Pyramid or the Giza necropolis, but it is generally assumed that it received its share of the restoration effort and that priests reopened Cheops's temples.

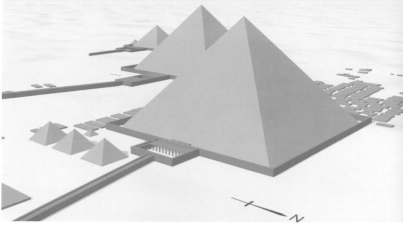

Strabo mentions that when he visited Egypt in 25 BC, the pyramid's entrance was closed with a huge stone. In time, wind-blown sand completely blocked its entrance.

Herodotus referred to the inscriptions that covered the outside of the pyramid. Even Arab travellers in the 12th century stated that the inscriptions on the faces of the pyramid could fill more than 10,000 pages. All these inscriptions vanished when the external limestone casing was removed in the 13th century. Since then, the pyramid has been as we see it today.

Herodotus does not say whether he entered the Great Pyramid. Probably not, otherwise such an eager observer would certainly have mentioned it. If he had entered he would have found an empty tomb, for it had been robbed 2,000 years before during the First Intermediate Period of the Seventh to the Tenth Dynasties.

Isometric drawing of the Giza Pyramids.

Arab Explorers

The Great Pyramid was reopened again in the year 820 AD by al-Mamun, the son of Khaliph Harun al-Rashid, who thought the building must contain treasure. For days he searched in vain for the entrance on the north face. As he did not want to be proved wrong, he decided to break through the casing stone in the hope of reaching one of the interior passages. With hammer and chisel, it proved impossible to break the stones; even with a blacksmith standing by continuously sharpening the tools. Finally, al-Mamun's men were able to break through the stone with a primitive but effective method. Close to the stones fire was ignited, and as soon as the stones glowed hot, cold acid was poured on them, until they split. In this way, they broke 30 metres into the core masonry of the pyramid. In this passage it was dark and there was little oxygen due to the fire they had ignited and the candles they were using. The air was also poisoned by the vapour of the acid they had poured on the hot stones. Al-Mamun was about to abandon the project when all of a sudden one of his workers heard the muffled sound of something heavy falling within the pyramid, on the left side of their passage. They started again with renewed enthusiasm, changing course towards the left side until they found a passage 110 centimetres wide and 120 centimetres high with a slope of 26°. On the ground, they found a huge prism-shaped stone that had fallen from the roof. They followed the passages and found the original entrance. When al-Mamun went down the passage to the subterranean chamber, he was astonished to find this small chamber roughly finished and vain of treasures. He turned his interest to the prism-shaped stone that had fallen from the roof. It appeared to him that this stone was plugging another passage that went up inside the pyramid.

Left: the Great Pyramid of Cheops: despite the makers' limited surveying tools no side varies more than 4.4cm in length from another, and the whole structure is perfectly oriented to the points of the compass. Until the 19th century it was the tallest building in the world and, at the age of more than 4500 years, it is the only one of the famous Seven Wonders of the Ancient World that still stands.

Top right: the first row of the pyramid's original casing at the northern face. It consisted of two-metre-thick polished limestone that glittered so brightly in the sun that it could be seen several kilometres away. At the middle of the southern face there are also a few blocks of the casing stones. This beautiful casing was stripped off in the Middle Ages to built Cairo houses.

Right: drawing of the Giza Pyramids from *Egypt, Descriptive, Historical and Picturesque* by Professor Georg Ebers, Leipzig, 1879.

At that moment, al-Mamun thought that he was on the edge of unfolding the secret of the pyramid. His men tried in vain to break the granite plug, then they also tried in vain to remove it. Al-Mamun, having in mind that he was going to reach undiscovered passages and chambers, ordered his men to cut in the core masonry and make a detour round the plugging stone. This task turned out to be more difficult than expected. As they destroyed a granite block 1.8 metres in length they found behind it another one, and behind the second one a third. They did not recount exactly how many granite plugs they found, but it is estimated that their number was more than twenty. Finally, they were able to crawl up a narrow ascending passage with a height of less than 120 centimetres, reaching a horizontal passage that ended in a rectangular chamber which they called the 'Queen's Chamber'. Eagerly, they stormed the 'Grand Gallery' and the 'King's Chamber' in the heart of the pyramid, but they were too late; thirty centuries too late. There was only an empty sarcophagus and nothing else. They knocked at every inch of the wonderful granite of the walls, listening for the echo of a free space or chamber. They also removed part of the floor's granite.

The precision with which the Great Pyramid was built is still, with today's technology, a source of great fascination. It is likely that the experimental phase of Cheops's father Pharaoh Snefru was the main driving force for this precision in work. This precision produced a pyramid whose base level difference in height is less than 2.1cm, and the maximum difference in length between the sides is 4.4cm. The blocks used in the pyramid have an average weight of 2.5 tons, decreasing in size towards the top. Some of the casing stones at the base are very large, weighing as much as 15 tons. The heaviest blocks are of granite, used as the roof of the King's Chamber and as weight-carrying support. Their weigh is estimated as 50 - 80 tons each.

In my opinion Cheops, who was able to undertake such vast work, was the most powerful human being that the world has ever seen.

Nineteenth-Century Explorers

Interest in the pyramids began to grow during the 18th century, but the climax of pyramid investigation was not reached until the 19th century. They were examined, drawn, measured and re-measured. Theories were put forth by a succession of Egyptologists including Caviglia, Belzoni, Vyse, Perring, Lepsius, Borchardt, Petrie and Reisner.

Among the early visitors, Giovanni Belzoni is an interesting figure. An Italian engineer living in Britain, Belzoni went to Egypt in 1815 to try to sell Mohamed Ali, the Viceroy of Egypt, a new hydraulic machine he had invented. In this he failed. So he decided to tour Egypt and remove its antiquities. Altogether, he spent five years in Egypt and Sudan. Then came the German archaeologist Lepsius who formed the 'growth theory' in 1843-1844. The theory stated that each Pharaoh added a certain amount to his pyramid during each year of his reign. This meant that the larger pyramids were built by the Pharaohs who had the longest reigns and vice versa. This theory, which has since been disproved, was reasonable compared with the fantastic notions put forth by some of the eccentric men who were at the time attached to the Giza Pyramids. According to these men, the buildings were all alleged to be observatories, temples, standard tables of measurement, anything but tombs. Lepsius honoured his Prussian king, Ferdinand Wilhelm IV, by making the Prussian flag fly on top of the Great Pyramid on the king's birthday. On this occasion Lepsius is quoted as saying: "At the top of the oldest and largest of all known human works, our flag with the Prussian eagle was unrolled, upon which we said thrice 'Long live the king!'" Lepsius published his famous book *Denkmäler aus Ägypten und Äthiopien*. However during his expedition he took 15,000 ancient pieces to Berlin.

In 1837-39, Howard Vyse and Perring, an energetic British pair, made a detailed survey of the Great Pyramid. John Taylor, also a Britain, who had never seen the pyramids, was a mathematician and an amateur astronomer. He took the Great Pyramid measurements of the French and also those of Howard Vyse, analysed

Left: the peak of the Great Pyramid. The present height is 137.38m, made up of 203 courses of masonry. The summit has a base length of 14.55m. The height of the pyramid as originally built was 146.649m. According to Rutherford the theoretical height of the pyramid was 147.807m.

Part of the pyramidion (see page 117) was found recently by Dr. Zahi Hawass.

Top right: the Great Pyramid viewed from north east.

Right: the eastern part of the ancient fence that surrounded the Great Pyramid.

them, and drew a few conclusions. He started to analyse the pyramid from a mathematician's point of view and tried to make a geometrical model. There was some confusion regarding the length of the pyramid's side. Successive travellers measured a greater side length. It occurred to him that each traveller measured accurately, but as more debris and sand were cleared from the base, each measurement came from a deeper layer of masonry. The first thing that drew his attention was that the pyramid's side makes a slope of 51°51′ to the horizontal instead of the regular angle of the equilateral triangle, which is 60°. Going back to Herodotus's story, he noticed what the priests had told him—that the sum of the vertical projection of the surface areas of the four faces equalled the square of the pyramid's height. At that moment he knew that the pyramid was of a unique geometrical design. Through further analyses, he showed that the ratio of the base perimeter to the pyramid's height equalled 2π. π is the ratio of a circle's circumference to its diameter, and is equal to $3.14159 \cong 22 / 7$. In other words, to state the above in a simplified description, the *height* of the pyramid has the same ratio to its *perimeter* as the *radius* of a *circle* to its *circumference*.

In addition, Taylor examined the pyramid's basic unit of measurement. The King's Chamber is 412.57 Imperial inches long and 206.28 Imperial inches wide. These are equal to 20 and 10 royal cubits (rc) respectively. A royal cubit is an Ancient Egyptian measuring unit, from which one measuring stick survives until today. The entrance passage is 41.26 Imperial inches wide, a width which is equal to 2 rc.

Further examination of the internal and external measurements showed that the pyramid builders also employed another unit of measurement, because of the frequent occurrence of the integral of the number 25.0265 Imperial inches. The natural conclusion is to assign this number as a basic unit of measurement used by the pyramid builders which was defined as a sacred cubit (sc). The big coincidence, however, is that the earth's polar radius is 250.265 million Imperial inches = 10 million sc. This means that the Pharaohs' unit of measurement was defined as one ten-millionth (1/10 million) of our Earth's radius. Further measurements inside the pyramid's chambers showed the necessity for a smaller unit of measurement which was defined as the primitive inch p′′, where 1 sc = 25 p′′ and 1 p′′ = 1.00106 Imperial inches. Without going into further details, the interior of the pyramid has various integer

Left: a view of the massive limestone blocks that form the Great Pyramid's core (eastern face). The smooth blocks of Tura limestone that once covered the pyramid were removed in the 13th century.

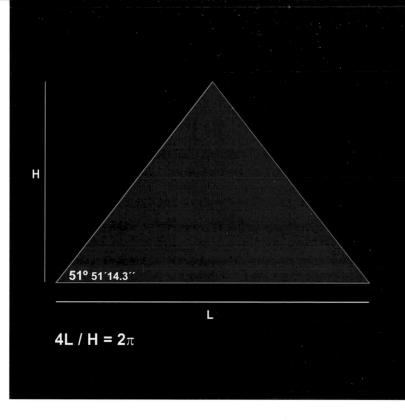

$$4L / H = 2\pi$$

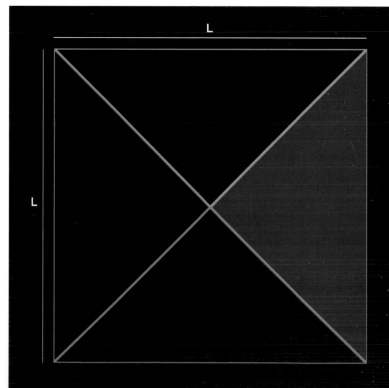

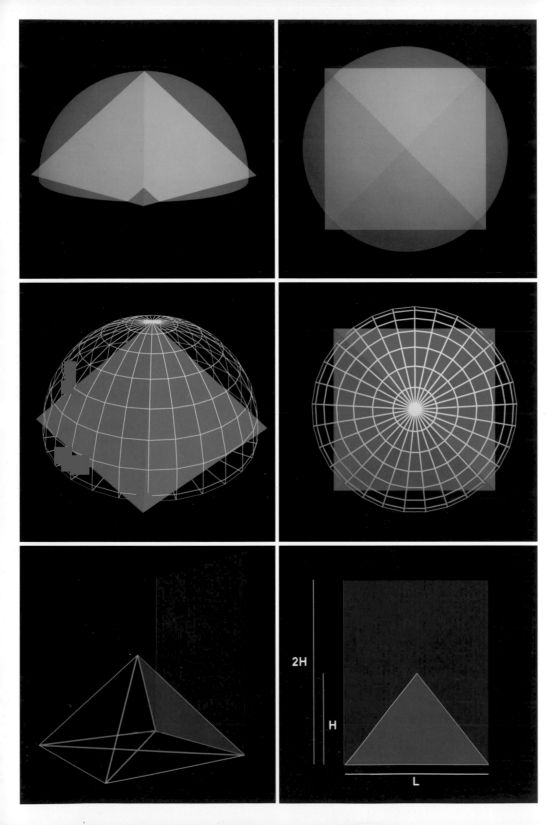

Taylor and Smyth reached the conclusion that the Ancient Egyptians, through their knowledge of π, were able to measure the width of one latitude degree and multiply it by 360 to calculate the earth's circumference at the equator. Furthermore, they found a hypotheses which stated that the Great Pyramid was a mathematical map of our planet's northern hemisphere *(left)*. The apex of the pyramid maps the earth at the north pole, the circumference of the pyramid's base maps the circumference of the earth at the equator. The height of the pyramid maps the polar radius of the earth.

Each face of the pyramid maps a quarter of the northern hemisphere, or a 90-degree spherical quadrant *(next page, top right)*. To map the quadrant on the pyramid's face (triangle) the quadrant's arc length must equal the triangle's side length and both figures must have equal height. This is only satisfied by considering a vertical projection of the pyramid's face (cross-section) and satisfying π ratio of the pyramid's height to its perimeter.

To simplify the above, consider the vertical projection of the pyramid's side which is a triangle of base L and height H. Its area equals ½ LH. The four sides of the pyramid have projections with a total area of 2LH. This area is equivalent to a rectangle on the pyramid's side with double the pyramid's height *(below left)*. This rectangle has the same area as a circle with radius the height of the pyramid *(below right)*. This enables us to draw a rectangle or a triangle that has an equal area with the correspondent spherical quadrant.

Rectangle area = 2H L
Circle radius = R = H
Circle area = π R² = π H²

Using the pyramid's π relationship
4L / H = 2π we can show that both the rectangle and circle have same area.

The pyramid base also maps onto the earth's diameter at the equator.

Earth's diameter = 2π R = 2π H
pyramid's perimeter = 4L = 2π H
⁻ Earth's diameter ⁻ 36,523.5 primitive inches
= 100 times the number of days in the year
1 p´´ (primitive inch) = 1.00106 Imperial inches

multiples of the primitive inch p′′. Alternatively, through a simple deduction, the primitive inch could be defined as (1/250 million) one two-hundred-and-fifty-millionth (1/250,000 000) of our Earth's polar radius.

At that moment, many questions occurred to Taylor: What could the definition of a primitive inch really mean? What could the Ancient Egyptians mean to express through the pyramid's measurements? He came to the conclusion that the pyramid was a model of our earth and solar year, with the dimensions of the Earth inherent in its geometry. However, Taylor's ideas were not accepted by the scientific community of his time. In 1859, he published a book entitled *The Great Pyramid, why was it built and who built it?*

After Taylor came Piazzi Smyth, a professor of astronomy from Scotland. He was very much impressed by Taylor's arguments and decided to visit Egypt to take the measurements anew. Armed with a whole set of surveying instruments, in addition to his skills in astronomy, he travelled to Egypt together with his wife in 1864. Through astronomical observation he obtained the exact geographical location of the pyramid on its summit, measuring the angle of slope of the pyramid's face as 51° 51′14.3′′. He also acknowledged the π relationship between the pyramid's height and base perimeter. Smyth adopted the same line of thought as Taylor, believing that there must be a clear mathematical link between the pyramid's dimensions and the Earth's basic geometrical data and astronomy. He pointed out that a projection of our planet Earth lies in the Great Pyramid. The apex of the pyramid maps the north pole, and the pyramid's perimeter maps the Earth's perimeter at the equator. Each face of the pyramid maps a quarter of the northern hemisphere, or a 90-degree spherical quadrant. To project correctly such a quadrant on a triangle (pyramid's face) the quadrant's arc length must coincide with the triangle's side length and both figures must have the same height. This is only satisfied by considering a vertical projection of the pyramid's face (cross-section) and satisfying π ratio of the pyramid's height to its perimeter. To state the above in a more simplified manner, and without complicated mathematics: draw a rectangle on the pyramid's side with double the pyramid's height. This rectangle has the same area as a circle with a radius the height of the pyramid. This enables us to draw a rectangle or a triangle that has an equal area with the correspondent spherical quadrant.

The pyramid's base perimeter measures 36,523.5 primitive inches. This number is also identical to 100 times the number of days in the year. Alternatively, each of the pyramid's sides measures 365.24 sc (1 sc = 25 p′′), which is also the number of days in

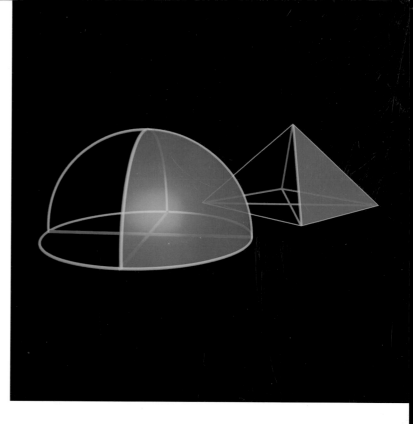

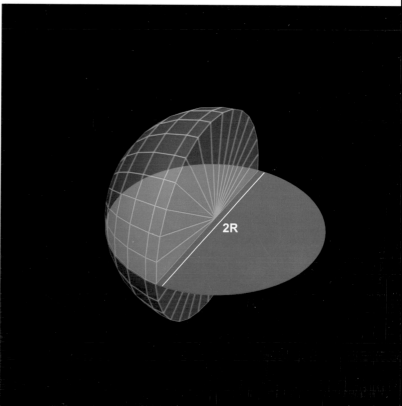

the year. Thus, Smyth's conclusion was that the Ancient Egyptians applied in the pyramid's geometry not only a linear measuring unit, but also a time measuring unit. How did the pyramid's designer intend this correlation? Smyth went further to state that the Great Pyramid was designed by the Deity Himself.

The man who blew these conclusion sky-high, while at the same time revealing the real wonder of the pyramids, was Sir Flinders Petrie. He did this by scientific measurement and precise mathematical calculation, spending three seasons at Giza, from 1880 to 1882, studying every inch of the site, carefully checking the orientation of the pyramids and measuring every dimension, inside and outside, with the most modern surveying instruments available at the time. The results were published in his *Pyramids and Temples of Gizeh*, which is now one of the standard works on the subject. Later, more accurate surveys were made. The orientation of the Great Pyramid is phenomenally accurate. The four sides are aligned almost exactly on the true north, south, east and west. In fact their orientation is so incredibly precise that compass errors can be checked against them. In 1925, S. H. Cole of the Survey Department of the Egyptian Government, using more accurate instruments than Petrie's, estimated the errors on each side as follows :

North Side	0° 2′ 28″ south of west
East Side	0° 5′ 30″ west of north
South Side	0° 1′ 57″ north of west
West Side	0° 2′ 30″ west of north

The maximum error was therefore only 5′ 30″, or a little over one-twelfth of a degree. On the south side the error was one-thirtieth of a degree. Who, one wonders, was the master engineer who planned and laid out this great building with such precision? And more importantly, how was it done? The magnetic compass was unknown to the Ancient Egyptians. They could of course have determined east and west approximately, by sightings

Left and right: Considered to represent the peak of the pyramid Age, the Great Pyramid is the ultimate of the knowledge and experience of all previous pyramids. Cheops grew up in an environment of the several pyramid building projects of his father, Pharaoh Snefru. Certainly the engineers, architects and organisers gained a lot of experience in the 'experimental phase' of Snefru. Hence Cheops had great advantage in being surrounded by these qualified men. Armed with this experience in addition of having great might and wealth and being regarded by his subjects as a divine ruler or god king, he was able to built this great monument. It is the only surviving item of the Seven Wonders of the World.

Top right is the southern face and *right* is the south east corner.

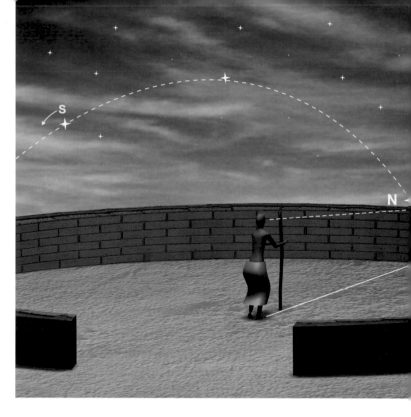

on the rising and setting sun on the equinoctial days; but in the words of I. E. S. Edwards (*The Pyramids of Egypt*) "the resultant error... would have been greater than the amount revealed by at least two of the main pyramids... " Edwards believed that the pyramid-builders may have determined east and west by "sighting on a star in the northern heavens and bisecting the angle formed by its rising position, the position from which the observation was made, and its setting position." For example, imagine a vertical rod driven into the ground and surrounded by a circular wall, the top of which is perfectly horizontal. By the rod stands a man, and near the wall, on the inside, is another man. A certain prominent star in the northern heavens has been selected for observation. When the man near the wall sees this star rising, he warns the man standing by the rod. As soon as the star rises above the rim of the wall the first man, sighting across the rod, takes a bearing on the star, and the second man marks its position on the wall. As the star travels across the sky, and as it sets 12 hours later, the same process is repeated and a second mark is made. This procedure would be repeated several times to check the accuracy of the observation. Then lines would be drawn joining the rod to the two points on the ground immediately below the marks. The line thus formed would be running north to south. The other two cardinal points would be at a right angle to it. This is a simplified explanation, but it will serve to show how the pyramids may have been oriented.

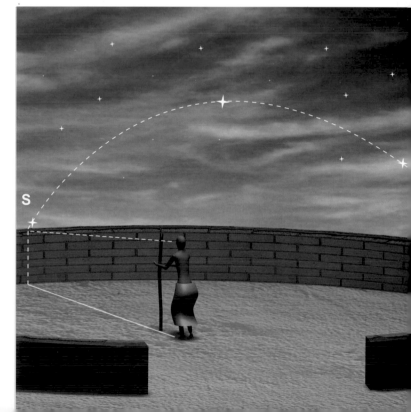

Finding the north by taking a sighting on a star in the northern sky. The observer marks on an artificial horizon the rising and setting the position of the star. In this experiment the artificial horizon is the top of a circular wall. The surveyor must be standing in the centre of the circle and he must not see beyond the wall.

The Great Pyramid's Measurements

Height	146.649 m
Present height	138.544 m
Side length: N side	230.251 m
E side	230.391 m
S side	230.454 m
W side	230.357 m
Average side length	230.356 m
Base perimeter	921.426 m
Displacement of entrance east of centre line	7.27 m
Face slope	51° 51′ 14.31″
Passage slope	26° 18′ 9.73″
Number of courses	203
Capstone height	9.26 m
Capstone's base length	14.54

A view of the south west corner of the massive limestone blocks that form the Great Pyramid's core. The smooth blocks of Tura limestone that once covered the pyramid were removed in the 13th century. The volume of the Great Pyramid is calculated as 2.6 million cubic metre.

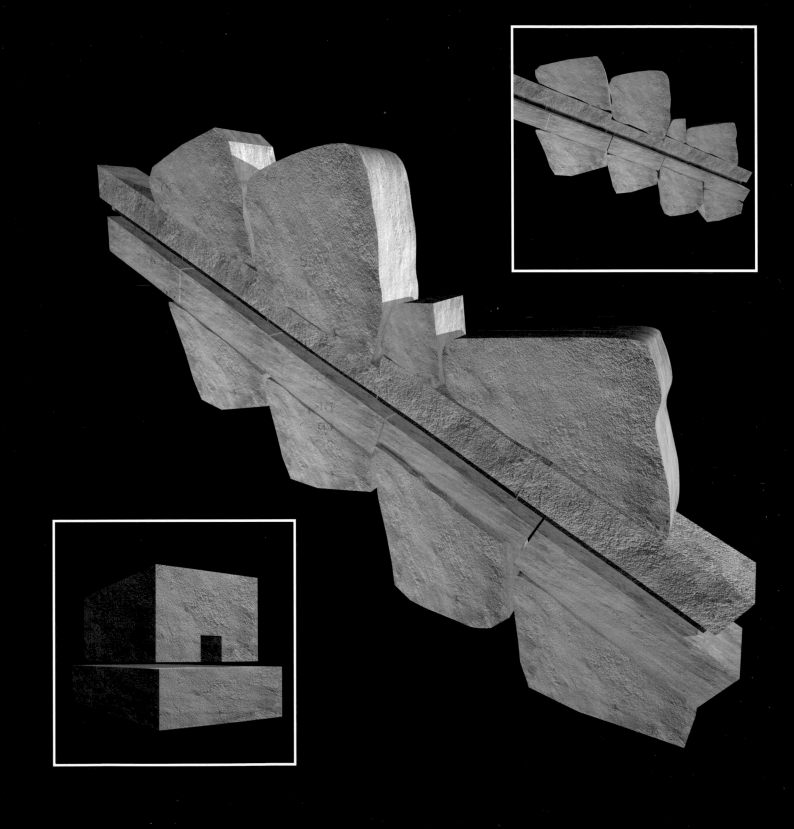

Air Shafts

The Great Pyramid of Cheops has four so called 'air shafts'. The King's Chamber has a northern and a southern shaft, and similarly the Queen's Chamber also has a northern and a southern shaft. The pyramid builders left the shafts of the King's Chamber open at both ends. However, the shafts of the Queen's Chamber were plugged at their entrance by an eight-centimetre stone and did not reach the pyramid's outer surface. The UPUAUT Project made an exciting discovery in 1993 by sending a robot through the entrance of the southern shaft of the Queen's Chamber. All four shafts are not straight.

The UPUAUT Project

Rudolf Gantenbrink, a German computer engineer, had a great interest in the technical aspects of archaeological issues. According to his own words, his engineering curiosity was aroused by the mysteries of the Great Pyramid. Furthermore, he said about the air shafts: "I was convinced that the shafts marked the first construction phase of the pyramid. They constitute basic elements of great importance. Put simply, a stone structure of such magnitude, built up in layers over a period of many years, is a sufficiently gargantuan undertaking to daunt any builder. But adding diagonal shafts through such a structure so complicates the task that it becomes a builders' nightmare. The builders must have ascribed great significance to the shafts, otherwise they would never have let themselves in for such a massive constructional headache." Gantenbrink worked in association with Professor Stadelmann, director of the German Archaeological Institute in Cairo. His first undertaking was to rediscover and clear the outlet of the southern air shaft of the King's Chamber. This air shaft had been discovered in the 19th century. He also installed an appropriate ventilation system at the exit of the southern shaft. The system controlled the humidity left by visitors in the King's Chamber. On average, the shafts measure 20.5 centimetres in width and 21.5 centimetres in height. Gantenbrink designed and built a robot which he called UPUAUT 1. In 1993 the robot was sent through the exits of the northern and southern shafts of the King's Chamber. It was found that both shafts had bends in the north-south axis. An improved ro-

Isometric drawing of the air shaft, which is approximately 20 x 20 cm in cross section. However to fit the shaft at an angular gradient between 30° and 50° through horizontally arranged layers of stone required two additional wedge-shaped blocks. Thus, each shaft sequence of cross-section 20 x 20 cm required the installation of four stones measuring in cross section 4 x 2 metres.

bot, UPUAUT 2, was sent from the entrance of the southern shaft of the Queen's Chamber. The robot was driven through for 65m until it was stopped by a blocking stone or door with two copper handles. This was an exciting discovery as every one's imagination suspected treasure behind the 'door with copper handles'.

In 2002, the National Geographic Society again sent a robot through the same air shaft, but this time equipped with a drilling machine. After drilling through the stopping stone with the copper handles it continued for a short distance until halted again by another stopping stone, also with copper handles.

The Air Shaft Mystery. In previous sections of this book, the development of the tomb in Ancient Egypt was explored. It started as a simple burial pit, then developed into the mastaba, then into the Step Pyramid, Bent Pyramid and finally the true pyramid. These evolutionary steps are very natural and were accompanied by a development in the religious cult. However, all previous and following pyramids had no air shafts. Gantenbrink and his team made a thorough study of the construction details of these shafts. The shafts' ceiling and walls were hewn from a single stone, and its floor was formed by a second stone (see drawings pages 93 and 94). To fit the shaft at an angular gradient between 30° and 50°, through horizontally arranged layers of stone required two additional wedge shaped blocks. Thus, each shaft sequence of cross-section 20 x 20 centimetres required the installation of four stones measuring in cross section 4 x 2 metres. The angular gradient of the shafts, in addition to their length as running through half of the pyramid, created many construction difficulties concerning the distribution of loads which the pyramid builders correctly solved.

Among the many suggested explanations for these shafts, archaeologists believe the most reasonable one would be that they were channels through which the Pharaoh's soul would ascend to the northern sky. However, this argument does not apply to the southern shafts, as religious tradition never associated the southern sky with the soul's ascent to heaven.

Left: the southern face of the Great Pyramid. The arrow points to the exit of the King's Chamber air shaft. Installed here is the ventilation equipment. The air shaft was originally discovered in 1872 by Dixon and newly rediscovered and cleared by the UPUAUT Project in 1993.

Top right: the north face of the Great Pyramid, showing the original entrance. It is located on the nineteenth row of blocks seven metres east of the centre of the northern face. The arrow points at the present entrance known as 'Mamun's Hole', which was forced by the Khaliph al-Mamun in the ninth century AD.

Right: the foundation socket on the north east corner.

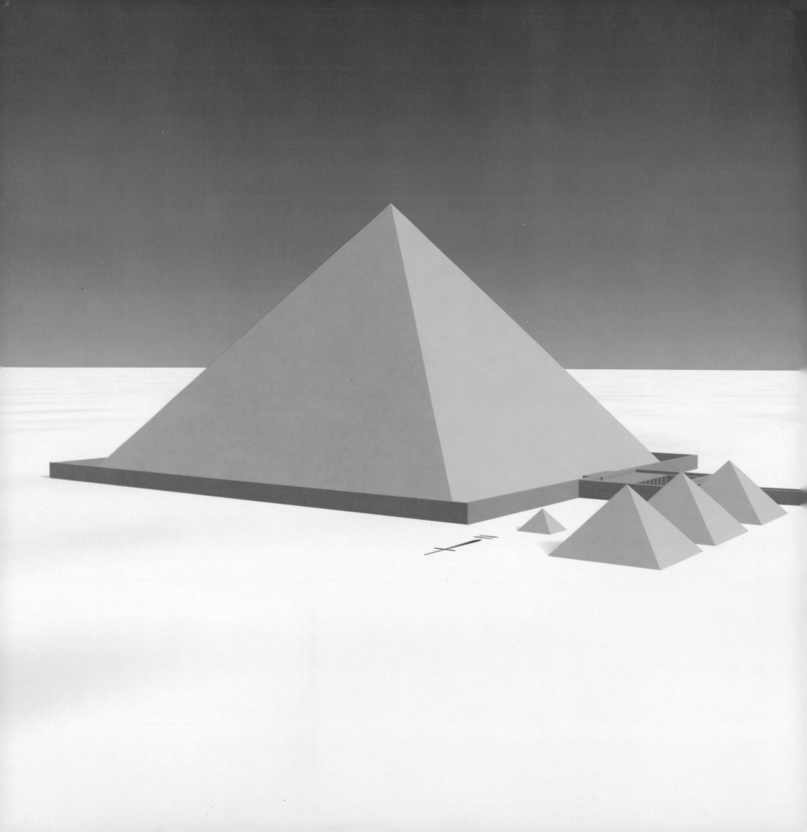

As a final word, although these shafts are small in dimension (20 x 20 centimetres), they could not be regarded as an 'insignificant architectural addition'. The builders must have made complicated calculations of weight and force distribution to allow the continuous flow of these diagonal channels through horizontal layers of masonry. Therefore, scholars assume that these shafts must have had an equally important religious significance.

Some Remarks on the Construction of the Great Pyramid

Due to the almost fanatical efforts of researchers, it can probably be claimed with every justification that the Great Pyramid is the most accurately surveyed building in the world. It has been estimated that the Great Pyramid is constructed of 2.3 million blocks of limestone, each weighing on the average 2.5 tons. The stones are arranged in 210 rows. The capstone or upper seven rows are missing, leaving 203 rows of stone. Most of the limestone of which the pyramids are built was quarried from the Mokattam hills, on the opposite bank of the Nile, and transported across by barges at flood time. The granite of the galleries and burial chamber came from Aswan in Upper Egypt.

Of the construction, Fakhry wrote: "If any special skill has disappeared, it is that of the organisers who supervised the timing of the various operations ... The process of quarrying, transporting, and erecting these monuments was an ordinary matter for the Ancient Egyptians, so they did not always consider it worthy of record. Most of the knowledge we have is based on the study of the monuments themselves." The description by Herodotus of how the blocks were raised in their position is confirmed by Petrie's investigations. As each course or layer of blocks was laid, a long ramp of earth and stones would be raised up to it, along which the blocks for the next course would be dragged. When the course was laid, the earth ramp would be raised, ready for the next course. The angle of slope did not change, so that the ramp would get longer and longer as work proceeded. The heavy blocks, each weighing several tons, would be manoeuvred into their final position by levers, machines formed from short wooden planks, mentioned by Herodotus. There is no mention in tomb drawings or elsewhere that the Ancient Egyptians possessed any machinery more elaborate than the lever, the roller and the inclined plane. Petrie described the method which may have been used in the construction.

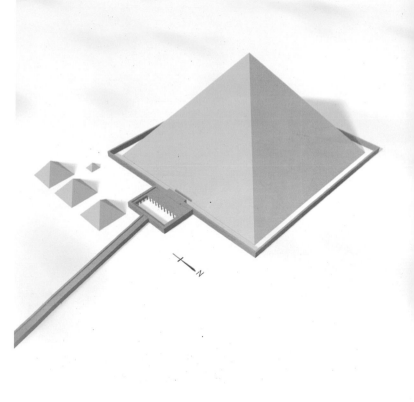

Left and right: a computer reconstruction of the Great Pyramid.

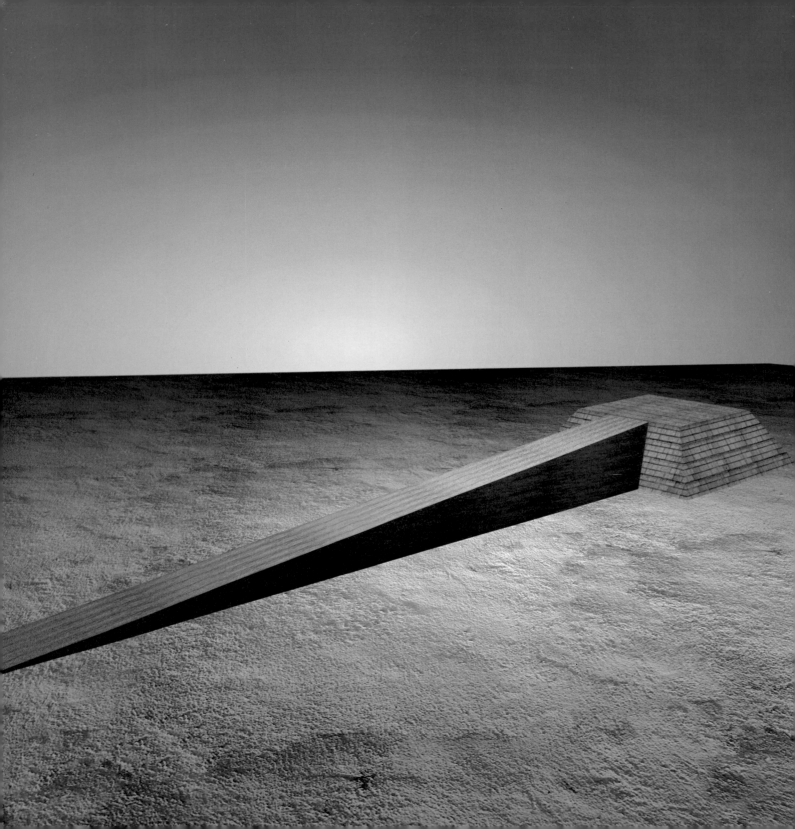

Even the largest blocks of the Great Pyramid, the 56 roofing beams of the King's Chamber, could have been raised by leverage, although they each weighed 54 tons. Petrie carefully examined some of the outer casing stones which originally covered the whole pyramid . There are still a few in position near the base (see picture page 77). The fineness of their workmanship was almost beyond belief. He wrote:

"... the mean thickness of the eastern joint of the northern casing stones is 0.020″ (1/50th of an inch), therefore, the mean variation of the cutting of the stone from a straight line is but 0.010″ (1/100th of an inch), of 75 inches up the face... These joints, with an area of 35 square feet each, were not only worked as finely as this, but cemented throughout. Though the stones were brought as close as 1/50th of an inch, yet the builders managed to fill the joints with cement, despite the great area of it, and the weight of stone, some 16 tons..."

The Ancient Egyptian workmen used bronze tools. The cutting joints of hard precious stone may have been of beryl, topaz, sapphire or hard uncrystallised corundum. For cutting the stones, they employed great bronze saws with jewelled cutting points. In some places, for example the granite sarcophagus of Cheops, the marks made by these saws can clearly be seen. By curving the saw-blades into a circle, drills were formed which could cut out a circular hole by rotation. For smaller objects, the cutting edge was held stationary while the work was revolved. "The lathe", says Petrie, "appears to have been as familiar an instrument in the Fourth Dynasty as in our modern workshops." Some of the superb diorite bowls must have been turned, as they are too accurate to have been made by hand. Though chisels have been found, no examples of jewelled saws and drills have been discovered, but this is not surprising as, owing to their value, they would have been carefully looked after and when worn, the jewels would have been removed and replaced.

Some 19th-century researchers came to the conclusion that the Great Pyramid's external measurements were correlated with our Earth's geometry. For this reason, the Great Pyramid became a constant source of inspiration to thoughtful men, who linked it with many mysteries and strange beliefs in astrology and spiritualism. Of the Giza Pyramids, only the Great Pyramid of Cheops is

The pyramid under construction. As the pyramid rose in height, the ramp rose in length and height to keep its gradient constant at 1 to 12. The supply ramp is made of bricks and debris, its purpose is to take the stone blocks up the pyramid. After the capstone was put on top of the pyramid the builders erected the casing stone and polished it from top to bottom, and at the same time they started dismantling the supply ramp.

the centre of attention of these theories. It is claimed its dimensions are the basis of many theories that predict the Old and New
Testaments. Others have gone still further to state that the Great
Pyramid was built by the Divine or Deity, and that it carries a blue-
print for destiny. All these theories claim that the Great Pyramid
was not built as the tomb of Cheops. For this they give supersti-
tious explanations which have all been rejected by historians.
Egyptologists have fiercely refuted all these mystical beliefs and
have further shown that the Great Pyramid is the natural development of the burial system. Archaeologists have also shown without doubt that the Great Pyramid is the tomb of Cheops. The
dimensions of its stones have no correlation with future events or
spiritualism. However, the pyramid's construction method, the
perfect alignment of its stones, its perfect alignment with Earth's
basic axis, and its dimensions are still not totally explained.
However, our lack of knowledge should not drive us to strange beliefs and rejection of archaeological evidence based on true historical events and facts.

Limestone statue of a seated scribe. The head is in proportion large compared with the body. The face is excellently sculpted. The eyes are inlaid,
with a copper line. The ornaments of the ear are also of copper. The statue
was found in Sakkara close to the seated scribe (see pages 24 & 25), Cairo
Museum.

Cheops, the Ingenious Pharaoh

Khufu, named Cheops in Greek, was the son of Pharaoh Snefru and Queen Hetepheres I, the daughter and heiress of Pharaoh Huni. Snefru ruled Egypt for more than 50 years, and during his reign built the pyramids at Dahshur and Meidum. His son Khnum-khuf, Khufu for short, chose the Giza Plateau in 2589 BC to build his Great Pyramid.

The Greek traveller Herodotus claimed that Cheops was a great but oppressive tyrant, who was hated by his subjects because he enslaved the whole country to build his Great Pyramid. Unfortunately, Ancient Egyptian stories do not support these claims. Cheops's era was to Herodotus as far away as Herodotus's time is to us. He must have been told these stories by some ignorant priests. In fact, Cheops was a charismatic ruler and in his reign art and building flourished. It is an error to judge history from a modern point of view. Cheops's era is to us so far away that we cannot apply our moral standards to evaluate him. We must not forget that he was divine, and that certainly his people were willing to participate in erecting his great monument. Had he been a hateful tyrant, he would have never left the country in such a wealthy and stable situation, one that enabled his son to build the Second Pyramid of Giza and the Sphinx. Cheops's funerary cult was also again popular in the Saite period (XXVIth Dynasty).

Herodotus also relates an old scandal concerning Cheops's daughter, who was said to have built a pyramid out of her immoral earnings (one stone from each man). This story suggests that Herodotus was talking to a dragoman. According to the Westcar Papyrus, Cheops liked to listen to fantastic stories of the reigns of his predecessors. The Westcar Papyrus, a copy of a papyrus dating from the Hyksos period, contains several stories originally written in about the 12th Dynasty. In it, he is portrayed as a good monarch, interested in the nature of human existence. His main concern was the construction of his tomb. The fourth tale in the Westcar Papyrus describes his search for "the secret chambers of the sanctuary of Thoth", which he wanted to produce in his own mortuary temple. On this occasion he consulted a magician from Meidum, 110

Despite Cheops's achievement of building his Great Pyramid, the only surviving statue of him is an ivory one 7.5cm long and found by Petrie at Abydos in 1903. During excavation at the Temple of Osiris at Kom al-Sultan close to Abydos one of his workmen brought him a headless statue of a man seated on a throne. From the hieroglyphic inscription Petrie immediately recognised that it was Cheops. He ordered all his men immediately to sift through the rubble that had been cast away in search of the head, offering a reward to the finder. Finally, after three weeks of intensive work, the head was found.

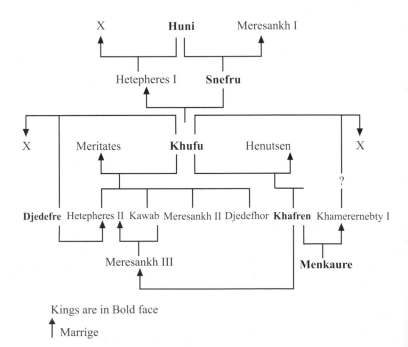

Kings are in Bold face

Marrige

years old, who ate 500 loaves of bread with meat, and drank 110 jugs of beer daily.

The vizier Hemon, a cousin of Cheops, was the Pharaoh's master of works and was responsible for the construction of the Great Pyramid. The impressive statue of Hemon from his tomb at Giza, now in the Hildesheim Museum, gives a magnificent portrait of this architect and engineer.

The only surviving likeness of Cheops is a small ivory one, 7.5cm long. It shows him seated on a cubic throne, dressed in a Shendyt kilt and wearing the Red Crown of Lower Egypt. The statue was found at Abydos by Flinders Petrie. An inscription in Wadi Maghara shows that Cheops continued his father's activity of mining in Sinai.

It is not clear how long Cheops's reign lasted. The Turin Canon, written 1,400 years after Cheops's death, claims that his reign lasted 23 years. But Manetho stated that his reign lasted 63 years.

Two of Cheops's sons succeeded him on the throne. Each of these sons was by a different wife. Kawab, Cheops's oldest son and heir to throne, he died during his father's reign without assuming even the title of a vizier. He was the first to be buried in the Giza necropolis. Kawab's wife was his half-sister Hetepheres. After his death she married another half-brother, Djedefre (or Radjedef), who succeeded Cheops on the throne. Cheops was preparing Kawab to be the heir to the throne and his sudden death must have been shocking to the father.

Djedefre was not among the legitimate line of successors, which probably divided the royal family. Much about Djedefre's reign is still unknown. But what we do know about him is that he moved the necropolis to Abu Rawash, where he built a small pyramid, now in ruins. He was also the first Pharaoh to include in his titles 'son of Ra'. The new ruler chose Abu Rawash to cut with the religious traditions of Cheops and to return to some Third Dynasty traditions, since this is where some Third Dynasty tombs lie. Djedefre also chose to build his pyramid on a rectangular ground plan like those at Sakkara. His pyramid and mortuary temple remained unfinished, which indicates that his reign was short. In 1901, Emile Chassiant found around the pyramid scraps of quartz (now in the Louvre Museum), which were originally 20 statues portraying the Pharaoh. These remains indicate they were some of the most magnificent statues of the Old Kingdom.

It was Djedefre who carved the first surviving statue of the royal sphinx. Probably the marvellous head of Djedefre found by Chassiant was originally part of a sphinx. Djedefre's pyramid at Abu Rawash was intentionally ruined in antiquity, which could have been the result of the royal family's conflict regarding his rule.

Meresankh III, the daughter of Kawab and Hetepheres II, married Chephren, Cheops's second son, who was next in line to the throne. There must have been a family struggle between the younger branch of Djedefre and the older branch of Chephren. The ascent of Chephren to the throne after Djedefre's temporary reign was considered a return to the traditions of Cheops. Chephren returned the royal necropolis to Giza, built his pyramid and valley temple, and carved the Great Sphinx.

The Giza Pyramids. The pyramids of Cheops, Chephren, and Mycerinus (foreground). Chephren's pyramid is built on slightly higher ground than the Great Pyramid of Cheops, and thus appears somewhat taller.

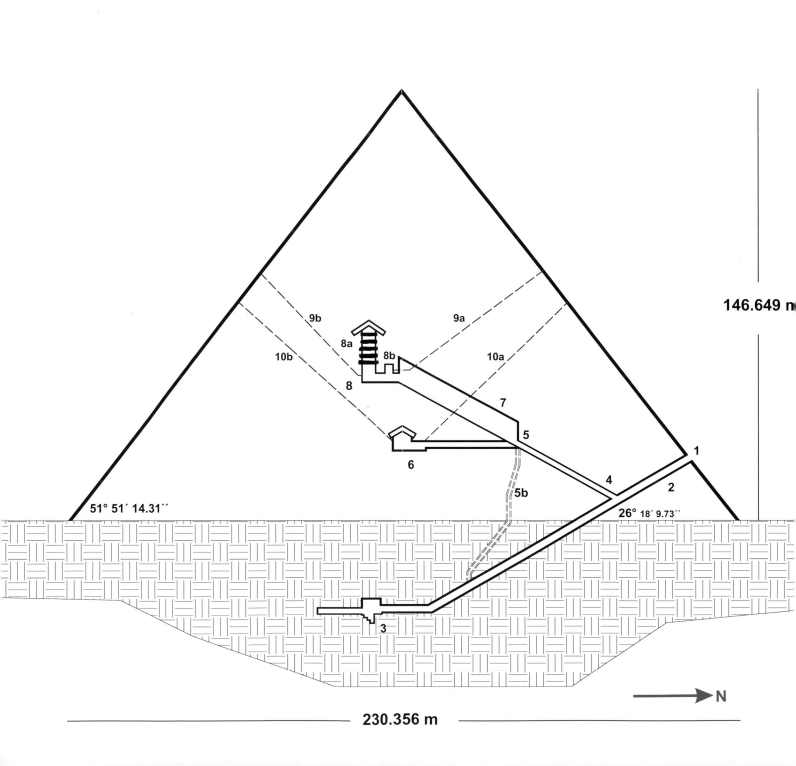

146.649 m

9b

9a

8a

8b

10b

10a

8

7

5

6

4

5b

51° 51′ 14.31″

26° 18′ 9.73″

3

230.356 m

N

Inside the Great Pyramid

Inside the Great Pyramid are neither decorations nor inscriptions; nonetheless, a visit to the burial chamber is worth the trouble. As in all pyramids, the entrance is on the north face. The present entrance is 17 metres above the base through the gap known as 'Mamun's Hole', which was forced by the Khaliph al-Mamun in the ninth century. It was cut in the sixth course of masonry, below and a little west of the original entrance (1); from there starts a descending passage (2) about 105 metres long with a slope of 26° 31′ 23′′, continuing horizontally for nine metres and leading into an underground chamber (3). This is the original burial chamber (subterranean chamber). This chamber is unfinished, and its walls are rough. In 1837 Vyse dug a 10-metre shaft in the eastern side of the subterranean chamber, which was slightly lower than the western side. He thought about what Herodotus had said about an underground tunnel linking the subterranean chamber to the valley near the Sphinx. In the south wall in front of the entrance is an opening with an unfinished passage. If this passage or corridor had been completed, it would have led to a second chamber. If this plan had been achieved, it would have been identical with Snefru's Northern Pyramid at Dahshur. However, at the Dahshur pyramid the second chamber lies below the apex of the pyramid. Here at Cheops's pyramid both chambers lie south of the apex. The descending passage is too narrow for a sarcophagus to pass through.

As this is now closed up, one passes through the present entrance to (4) and from there climbs the narrow, steep ascending passage for its 39-metre length. The entrance of the ascending passage was covered with a limestone slab, making it identical with the remaining roof. It was this limestone slab that fell when

Right: a cross section of the King's Chamber showing the stress-relieving chambers of roughly cut blocks of red granite. The ceiling of the King's Chamber is made up of nine granite slabs, each five metres long. Above them five compartments were formed (8a) to relieve the enormous strain on the ceiling. Each has the same area as the respective chamber below. It is estimated that each granite slab weighs 50-80 tons. The upper slab has a pointed shape, while the four lower slabs are flat. The height of the whole structure from the upper slab to the floor is approximately 21m. This ingenious design had not been used before in any pyramid. Quarry marks on some of the stones in these chambers mention the names of the workmen and the 17th year of Cheops's reign, which means that the pyramid had reached this stage at that time. Each of the granite slabs has cracks, which were probably due to earthquakes. The fact that these stress-relieving chambers have withstood the loads for more than 45 centuries is explained by their ingenious construction.

1. Entrance
2. Descending passage
3. Subterranean chamber
4. Ascending passage
5. Entry to the Grand Gallery
5b. Escape shaft
6. Queen's Chamber
7. Grand Gallery *(see pages 111 - 115)*
8a. Stress-relieving chambers above the King's Chamber.
8b. The antechamber with three stopping stones *(see pages 114 - 115).*
8. King's Chamber
9a. Northern air shaft in the King's Chamber.
9b. Southern air shaft in the King's Chamber.
10a. Northern air shaft in the Queen's Chamber.

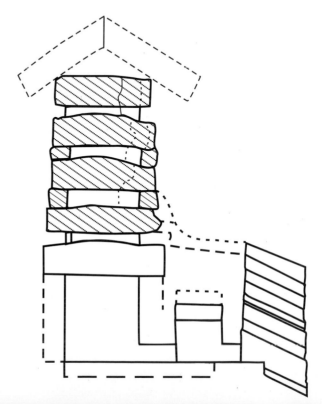

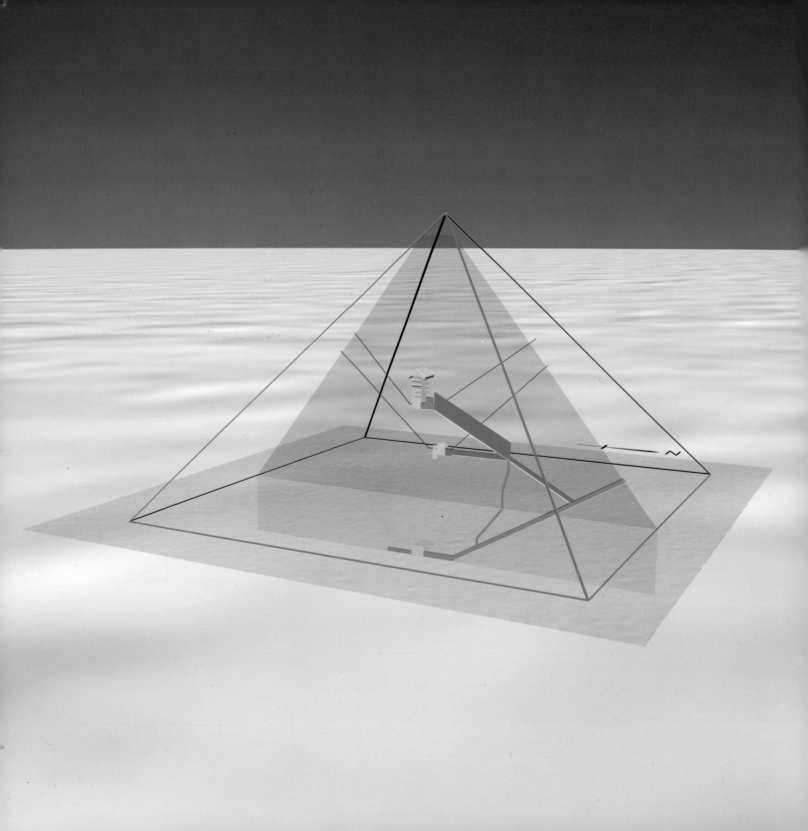

al-Mamun's men were digging their hole. The ascending passage is so low that the visitor is obliged to walk nearly double (handrails and electric lighting make this less arduous). It has an ascending slope of 26° 2′ 30′′, which is nearly identical to the slope of the descending passage. At (5) one can walk upright, and there a passage branches off to the Queen's Chamber (6).

Egyptologists think that the Great Pyramid underwent several changes during its construction. After finishing the Subterranean Chamber (3), the builders decided to enlarge the building. So they augmented in the construction the ascending passage (4) to (5), which terminates in the Queen's Chamber (6). In fact, this was the new burial chamber after the enlarged plan. At (5) is an opening, the escape shaft, which descends with a sheer angle to a depth of 60 metres. It reaches the descending passage, and it is now accepted that this was an escape shaft for the priests who closed the ascending passage with enormous stones after the Pharaoh's mummy had been laid inside. Once the stones had been dropped off in the ascending passage it would have been completely blocked, and the priests would have been trapped inside. The only exit was by the escape shaft and then by walking up the descending passage to the entrance (2). When the last priests left the pyramid 4,600 years ago, the entrance of the ascending passage must have been not only completely blocked, but also indistinguishable from the rest of the roof.

It has been pointed out above that al-Mamun's men found the entrance of the ascending passage blocked by three granite stones which they could not break, and that they therefore made a detour by cutting through the core masonry. These blocking stones are still in place today. Petrie found that their size was larger than in any of the passages, and they could only be accommodated in the Grand Gallery (7). This would interfere with funeral rituals, but there is no other place that could hold these stones.

Before completing the Queen's Chamber (6), the builders decided for the second time to enlarge the building and build a third and higher burial chamber. Its floor remained rough. At (5) one goes up the steps and reaches the Grand Gallery (7), 46.7m long and 8.7m high. This is actually a continuation of the ascending passage. The polished limestone on the walls rises to a height of 2.25 metres. Above this are seven rows of stone, each row seven centimetres in from the row below it. The Grand Gallery is a passage; it is the most wonderful and impressive feature inside the

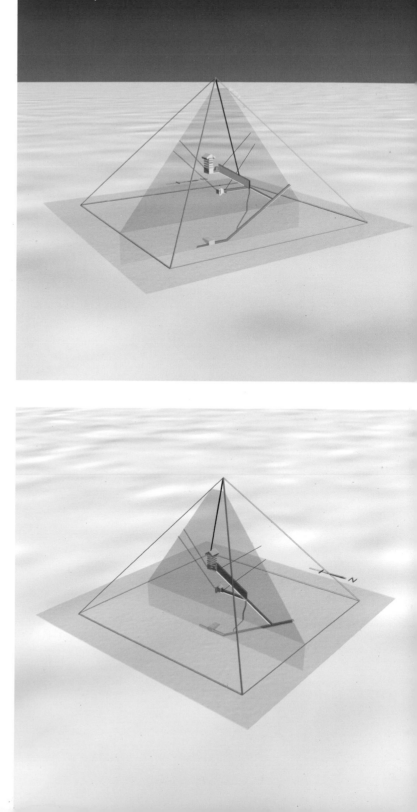

The chambers and passages inside the Great Pyramid. All passages coincide with the orange 'hyper plane'. It is displaced by 7.27m towards east from the centre of the northern face. The light orange 'plane' is continued below ground.

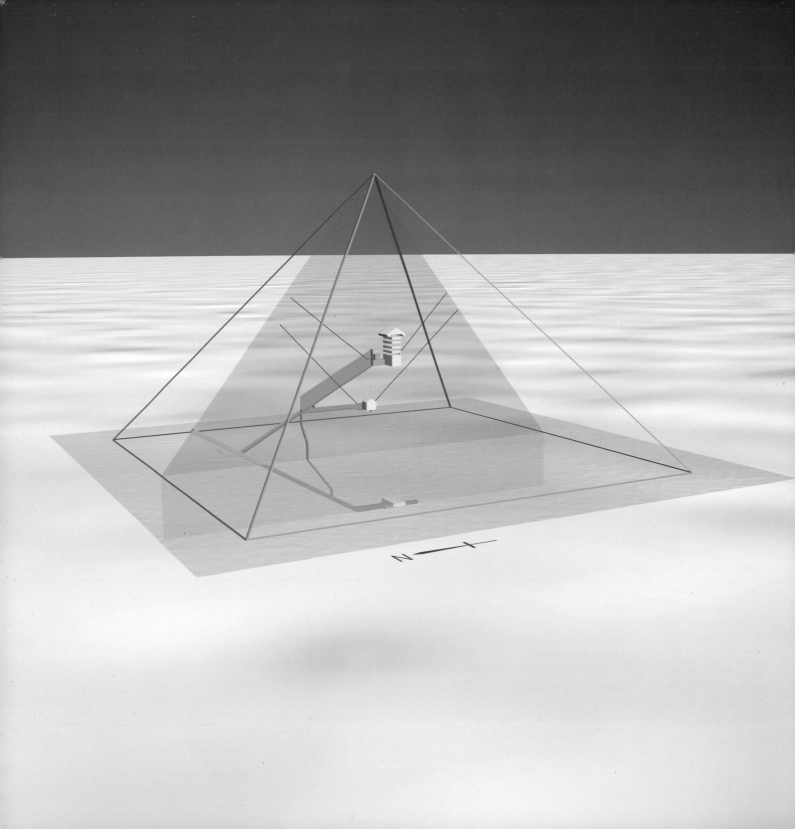

Great Pyramid. On the stairs, now furnished with handrails, one climbs to the end of the gallery and there reaches a small passage just over one metre high and about seven metres long. After climbing a high step one reaches the antechamber (8b). Four wide openings are hewn in the east and west walls of this chamber *(see pages 114 and 115)*. Borchardt says that blocking stones were lowered into these openings by means of ropes. The purpose of these blocking stones was to prevent access to the King's Chamber. Nothing of these blocking stones was found.

The antechamber leads to the burial chamber itself, also called the King's Chamber (8), which lies nearly 42 metres above ground level. It is 10.8 metres long with its axis from west to east, 5.7 metres high and 5.2 metres wide. Nine granite slabs, each five metres long, form the ceiling; above them five compartments were formed (8a) to relieve the enormous strain on the ceiling. Each has the same area as the respective chamber below. It is estimated that each granite slab weighs 50 - 80 tons. The upper slab has a pointed shape, while the four lower slabs are flat. This ingenious design had not been used before in any pyramid. Quarry marks on some of the stones in these chambers mention the names of the workers and the 17th year of Cheops's reign, which means that the pyramid had reached this stage at that time. Each of the granite slabs has cracks, which were probably caused by earthquakes. The chamber itself is of granite; it should be noted how the granite blocks are so closely fitted in the walls as to make them appear almost seamless. The granite sarcophagus, two metres long, one metre high and just under one metre wide, was empty when discovered. The sarcophagus is roughly made, and has clear marks of saw cutting. The sarcophagus is wider than the entrance of the chamber, and must therefore have been put in its place during the building of the pyramid. Up to the present time the mummy of the Pharaoh has not been found; nor is it known what became of the lid of the sarcophagus. Archaeologists think that the tomb was robbed at the fall of the Old Kingdom, during the time of unrest called the First Intermediate Period.

The northern and southern walls of the King's Chamber each have an air shaft (9). However, these so-called air shafts must have had a religious significance related to the soul of the Pharaoh. They must have been formed to give way for the Pharaoh's soul to ascend to heaven. The northern air shaft has an angle of 31°, the southern air shaft, pointing to Orion, has an angle of 45°. For more details, refer to the section on air shafts and the UPUAUT project.

Left: the interior of the Great Pyramid.
Right: illustration of the Grand Gallery.

Modern archaeologists have another point of view, which states that all three chambers were planned from the beginning and that there was no modification in plan. The so-called Queen's Chamber was a *serdab* or a closed room for the *ka* statue, the Pharaoh's spiritual double. This is the same model as Djoser's statue in the stone enclosure at the Step Pyramid. The King's Chamber is the actual burial chamber. The subterranean chamber in its rough state would symbolise the underworld cavern of the god Sokar. Furthermore, it is likely that the subterranean chamber was not the first to be built but rather the last, and therefore it remained unfinished. Alternatively, the subterranean chamber could be a sort of backup tomb to be used in case the Pharaoh died before the completion of the pyramid.

Originally the air shafts in the Queen's Chamber did not open through the walls. But since the air shafts existed in the King's Chamber, Smyth went on knocking on the walls and listening to the echo until he found and opened the air shafts. The two air shafts point to the north and south. The northern one points to the Polar star, the southern one to Orion.

Miroslav Verner thinks that the Queen's Chamber was intended to serve as a backup burial chamber. The builders knew what a dangerous and risky task lay ahead of them in building the Grand Gallery and the King's Chamber. Nothing like it had ever before existed, and they could not estimate either the difficulties involved or how long it would take to complete the project.

Miroslav Verner adds "Perhaps it was for this reason that the Queen's Chamber was kept ready, and lost its function only after the completion of the saddle ceiling in the highest stress relieving chamber over the King's Chamber. At that time, the air shafts in the Queen's Chamber, whatever their significance, were ritually sealed. It is worth noting that the 'stopper stone' in the south shaft of the Queen's Chamber is located about the level of the vertex over the highest relieving chamber over the King's Chamber."

On the Pyramid's south face at the height of the 35th course of masonry you will see a hollowing in the masonry. This is the result of the blast made in 1836 by Richard Howard Vyse, who thought he would discover the entrance to Cheops's treasure. All pyramids have entrances on the northern side.

The Grand Gallery furnished with modern hand rails and staircase.

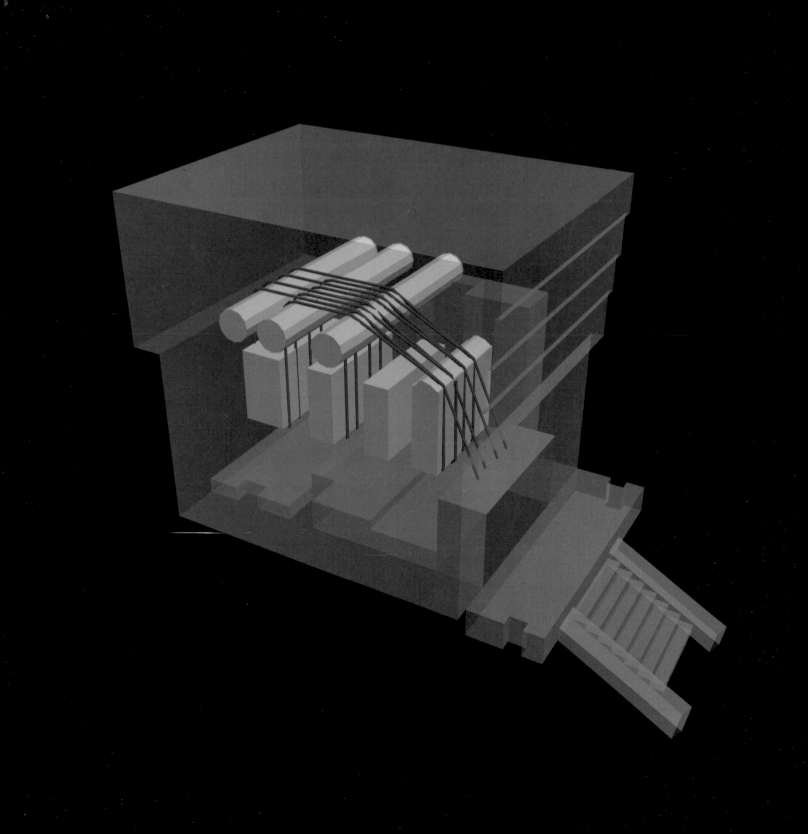

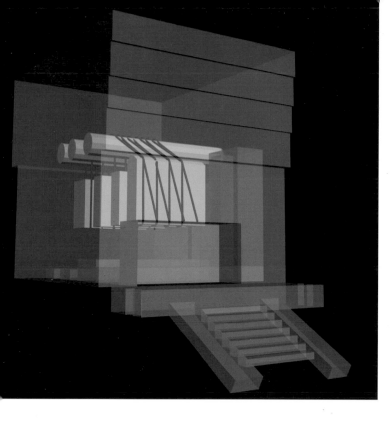

Left and above: the three granite stopping stones in the antechamber between the Grand Gallery and the King's Chamber. When the priests left the King's Chamber for the last time *c.* 4,600 years ago they cut the ropes, allowing the three granite slabs to slide down and close the King's Chamber as a first protection.

Right: drawing of the Grand Gallery from *Egypt, Descriptive, Historical and Picturesque* by Georg Ebers, Leipzig, 1879.

Sites Around the Great Pyramid

Solar Boats. Three boat pits cut into the rock lie around the mortuary temple on the Great Pyramid's eastern face. All were found empty by George Reisner. Facing the south side is a modern boat-shaped building. This marks the fourth boat pit discovered in 1954 by Kamal al-Malakh. This pit, rectangular and not boat-shaped, contained a complete dismantled solar boat. It has been reassembled and lies in a modern building, the Solar Boat Museum. The boat has a total length of 43.2 metres. Beyond it, lies the fifth pit containing another dismantled boat.

Foundation Sockets. At the north-eastern corner you will see one of the four foundation sockets of the pyramid (see picture on page 95). It is a rectangular cavity in the rocks, approximately 3.5 metres across and a few centimetres deep. Foundation sockets were used to establish the pyramid's diagonals and sides, but the pyramid never reached these corners. Also very distinguishable is the north-western socket. The first impression the observer gets is that the pyramid never reached as far as the sockets unless the finished casing was also at each face. In fact, the four faces of the Great Pyramid are concave by about a metre deep. With the normal eye this concavity is invisible since it is distributed over the length of the side, 232 metres.

Hetepheres I's Tomb. Queen Hetepheres I was the wife of Snefru and mother of Cheops. Her tomb was discovered intact in 1925 by George Reisner is, and is the only royal tomb to have survived from the Old Kingdom. The tomb contained her royal furniture (now in the Cairo Museum), canopic chest and the queen's

In the Old Kingdom it was customary to bury funerary boats near the burial monument. A number of empty boat-shaped pits occur around the Great Pyramid. In 1954 Kamal al-Malakh discovered two intact boats on the south side of the pyramid. The pit was closed by 41 limestone blocks, each weighing 16 tons, and completely sealed with plaster. A smaller keying block at one end had to be removed, before any of the larger ones could be lifted. The pit is rectangular and not boat-shaped.

When opened, two dismantled cedarwood boats were discovered, the oldest boats of that size to be found so far. The pit was 30m long, and the boat after it had been assembled was 43.2m long. A large cabin was placed a little after midship on the deck, its roof supported by palm-shaped columns. The timber was held together by wood pins and ropes. Ahmed Youssef was responsible for the ingenuous work of restoring and reassembling the vessel. He was also responsible for much of the work on the furniture of Queen Hetepheres.

The burial of the boats was performed by Cheops's successor Djedefre. An inscription on the blocks reads 'Re-djed--ef is the ruler'. This must have been carried out by some of the workmen.

alabaster sarcophagus. The canopic chest, in which the viscera were normally placed after removal from the body during the process of mummification, still contained the queen's internal organs. This is one of the most important discoveries in the history of mummification since it is the earliest proof of removal of the viscera. However, there was nothing of the Queen's mummy. She was probably buried near one of the two pyramids of Snefru at Dahshur. Presumably, thieves entered her tomb during her son's reign, so it was decided to bring her funerary furniture, including her alabaster sarcophagus, for reburial at the bottom of a deep shaft east of the Great Pyramid. The mummy of the queen and her jewellery have not yet been found.

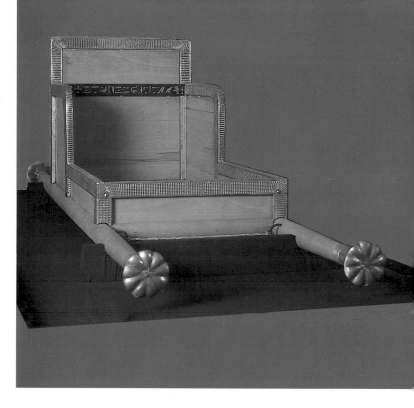

Today the visitor can see the furniture in the Egyptian Museum, exactly in the same state as the queen had it in her life. Under the gold canopy, which her husband Pharaoh Snefru gave her, stands the bed in which, perhaps, her son Cheops was born. Beside it stands her gold-encased armchair and her carrying chair with its gold handles. Her carrying chair bore an inscription inlaid in gold hieroglyphs set in ebony panels, giving her name and titles as 'Mother of the Pharaoh of Upper and Lower Egypt, Follower of Horus, she who is in charge of the affairs of the harem, whose every word is done for her, daughter of the god, of his lions, Hetepheres'. Nearby is her make-up box with its neat alabaster jars in position, and her jewellery box containing her silver anklets. No one who has had the opportunity to see this furniture is likely to forget its strength, simplicity and grace. These furniture pieces are a clear sign of the excellent craftsmanship and artistic standard reached in the Fourth Dynasty.

Mortuary Temple. In front of the east face of the Great Pyramid are the ruins of the mortuary temple. Today nothing remains of the temple itself, and only its foundation can be seen. Its measurements were approximately 40 x 50 metres. Remains of the causeway can still be recognised leading east towards the modern

Left and top right: the magnificent furniture of Queen Hetepheres, mother of Pharoh Cheops, found by George Reisner in 1925 inside a 33m-deep shaft near the Great Pyramid. It is the only royal furniture that survived intact from the Old Kingdom. Also found in the shaft was an empty sarcophagus and a canopic chest containing the viscera of the Queen. Buried also were some objects used by the queen in her lifetime such as gold and alabaster vases, rings, knives and a manicure set, as well as her bed and two armchairs covered in gold. Her sedan chair *(top right)* has a gold inscription inlaid in ebony. The inscription reads: 'The mother of the King of Upper and Lower Egypt, Follower of Horus, she who is in charge of the affair of the harem, whose every word is done for her, daughter of the god, of his lions Hetepheres'.

Right: boat pit east of the Great Pyramid.

village of Nazlet el-Samman. Lepsius says that he found the causeway intact. Modern archeologists believe that Cheops's valley temple lies below Nazlet al-Samman.

Cheops's Satellite Pyramid. Facing approximately the middle of the east side is a ramp hewn in the rocks. At first sight it appears as the entrance of a tomb. However, it is a trial passage which the pyramid builders cut in the rock; an exact replica of the Pharaoh's burial passages. It has the same angle of descent, ascent and dimensions. Zahi Hawass, however, is of the opinion that this is not a trial passage but one that belongs to Cheops's satellite pyramid. Due to the plan of enlarging the mortuary temple, the pyramid was then built further south. This small satellite pyramid built for Cheops's *ka*, with sides measuring 20m, was discovered by Zahi Hawass. Here are also three small pyramids which Cheops built for his queens.

The Pyramidion. South of the satellite pyramid Zahi Hawass found a large limestone block with three sloping sides. This block was the base of the pyramidion. One side of it must have been missing. A year latter the remaining parts of the pyramidion were found lying on the north side of the Great Pyramid.

Left: from a civilisation long disappeared, the three Giza Pyramids stand in breathtaking geometrical symmetry. In the foreground before Mycerinus's pyramid, the smallest of the three, are the satellite tombs of his family. Chephren's pyramid (centre), with its original limestone casing still partly in place, appears larger than the Great Pyramid to the rear because it is built on a higher ground.

Top right: the newly-discovered pyramidion, now on display on the east side of the Great Pyramid.

Right: the trial passage east of the pyramid (see text above).

The Pyramids of Chephren and Mycerinus

The funerary complexes of the Fourth Dynasty Pharaohs Chephren (2558-2532 BC) and Mycerinus (2532-2504 BC) are unique among Old Kingdom pyramid sites in their completeness. Chephren's complex, with its pyramid, mortuary temple and valley temple, gives us a comprehensive picture of an Old Kingdom royal burial. Systematic excavations of this site were first carried out by Auguste Mariette in the middle of the 19th century. Among several fragments that had fallen into a shaft, he discovered a statue of Chephren which is considered one of the most magnificent monuments of the Old Kingdom. The statue, now in the Egyptian Museum in Cairo, shows Chephren seated on the royal throne protected by the dynastic god Horus, who enfolds his wings around the nape of Chephren's neck.

Pyramid of Chephren, Great is Khafre

The second largest pyramid of the group was built in 2550 BC by the Pharaoh Chephren (Khafre in Ancient Egyptian). It lies to the south-west of Cheops's pyramid, on the prolongation of the diagonal of that structure. To the Ancient Egyptians it was known as Wer-Khafre, meaning 'Khafre is Great'.

In size it is not quite so overpowering as that of Cheops, but since it is built on higher ground it appears even larger, especially when viewed from the southern, desert side. Each side measured 215 metres, but is now 211 metres long, and inclined at an angle of 53° 7′.

The pyramid of Cephren can be neither climbed nor entered. To the south is a small pyramid, the tomb of the queen, and to the east lies the mortuary temple, now in almost complete ruin. From there, a causeway leads to the Temple of the Sphinx or Granite Temple. The pyramid's height is 144 metres, and it retains virtually its full height by the preservation of the limestone casing at the building's apex. The lowest course of the pyramid's 'outer skin' is composed of red granite blocks, best preserved at the western end of the south side.

Left: the Pyramid of Chephren; its base side was 215 m, rising to a height of 143.5m at an angle of 53° 7′.

Right: sunset at Chephren's pyramid.

Right: the Giza Pyramids.

Pharaoh Chephren

Chephren was the son of Pharaoh Cheops and Queen Henutsen, and followed his elder half-brother Pharaoh Djedefre to the throne. It is not known why he succeeded by his half-brother, but it is possible that none of his former Pharaoh's sons had survived and that Chephren thus was the oldest surviving male descendant of their father Cheops.

The Turin canon records a rule for him of more than 20 years, but according to Manetho and Herodotus it was 66. Today it is generally accepted, however, that he ruled for about 26 years, possibly a few more. It is thought that during his reign there was a restoration of Cheops's traditions. The solar-religion grew in importance and, like his brother before him, Chephren adopted the title 'Son of Re', a tradition that would last for over a millennium.

Chephren returned the royal necropolis to Giza, built his pyramid and valley temple and carved the Sphinx. The priest Manetho mentions that Bauefre succeeded Chephren, and it is most likely that Bauefre built the unfinished pyramid at Zawiyet al-Aryan. But the next Pharaoh was Menkaure, also a son of Chephren. Herodotus named him Mycerinus. Manetho is unsure of the length of Mycerinus's reign; he thinks it was 18 years. The next Pharaoh was Shepseskaf, the last Pharaoh of the Fourth Dynasty.

Left and top right: the Pyramid of Chephren.
Right: funerary monument of Queen Khentkawes.

Valley Temple of Chephren

Close to the Sphinx lies the best-preserved valley temple at Giza. From here in ancient times a sloping causeway led to the mortuary temple in front of Chephren's pyramid. The temple was 45m long and 13m high, and its beauty lay in the simplicity of its proportions. It was discovered in 1853 during the clearing of accumulated sand from the Sphinx under the direction of the French Egyptologist Auguste Mariette. Here Mariette also found the statue of Chephren which is now in the Egyptian Museum. Analysis of the stone blocks of the valley temple showed that they were quarried from the chest of the Sphinx.

In the T-shaped hall of this valley temple the final funeral ceremonies were conducted before the coffined corpse of the Pharaoh was taken along the causeway to his pyramid. This hall is one of the most impressive interiors that the Old Kingdom builders have left us. Light diffused from the inclined openings cut in the tops of the walls where they met the roof, and fell on the polished alabaster floor, reflecting a diffused light on the 23 statues of the Pharaoh made of green diorite and grey schist that stood at intervals along the walls.

Inside the Pyramid of Chephren

The Pyramid of Chephren has two entrances, each leading to a descending corridor that ends in a chamber. The lower passage begins 68m north of the pyramid and was totally cut through the solid rock of the plateau. It joins the upper corridor by an ascending passage. The lower passage has a slope of 21° 40′, but becomes horizontal for a short distance before rising steeply to meet the upper corridor. The lower entrance was abandoned in favour of the upper entrance. The upper corridor has a descending slope of 25° 55′. The reason for building the upper passage and neglecting the lower one is unknown. It has been suggested that after building the lower entrance, the architect decided to build the whole pyramid further south. Part of the upper corridor is hewn in the rock. The wall and roof of the corridor are covered with red granite; the corridor leads to the burial chamber containing a red granite sarcophagus. The length of the chamber is 14m from west to east, its width is five metres from north to south and it is seven metres in height. Two other passages in the pyramid are the work of ancient thieves. Rectangular shafts, similar to the air shafts of the Great

Left: the upper courses of fine limestone remain, so that the pyramid has not lost any of its original height 143.5 m.

Right: statue of Chephren, Cairo Museum.

127

Pyramid, were cut on the northern and southern walls of the burial chamber to a depth of only half a metre, but were abandoned. Squares marked in red, approximately 1.5m below the present cavities, suggest that this was a previous plan that had been abandoned in favour of the above cavities.

A chamber measuring 11 X 3.5m is situated in the middle of the horizontal passage described above. Archaeologists believe that this must have been where, according to the original plan, the burial chamber was situated. Then, for some reason, the construction of the whole pyramid was shifted south by about 68m. It is a custom in all pyramids to have the entrance in the north face, and to have the burial chamber beneath the apex. The reason for shifting the construction site south could have been to create direct access to the causeway and avoid the Sphinx rock. However, this argument does not explain why the two entrances were connected by an ascending shaft, especially in that this shaft was later closed with blocking stones by the builders.

The remains of the queen's pyramid lie near the pyramid. The mortuary temple is built of limestone and has an entrance hall, an open court, five niches for statues, magazines and a sanctuary. Around the temple are five boat pits. A small track 500 metres long connects the mortuary temple and the valley temple. The valley temple, a square building with two entrances, is the best-preserved building from the Fourth Dynasty.

Giovanni Belzoni was the first to enter the inside of Chephren's pyramid in modern times (between 1816 and 1820). His accounts of this adventure are worth quoting:

"My undertaking was of no small importance; it consisted of an attempt to penetrate into one of the Great Pyramids of Egypt, one of the wonders of the world. I was confident that a failure in such an attempt would have drawn on me the laughter of all the world for my presumption in such a task; but at the same time I consider that I might be excused, since without attempting we would never accomplish anything."

First Belzoni studied the south side of Chephren's pyramid.

"I examined every part and almost every stone. I continued to do so on the west, then I came round to the north side. Here the appearance of things became to my eyes somewhat different from that at any of the other sides. The constant observation I made on the approach to the tombs at Thebes perhaps enabled me to see what other travellers had not; indeed, I think this ought to be considered as a standing proof that in many cases practice goes further than theory."

Isometric drawing of the Pyramid of Chephren.

Belzoni had employed peasants to clean the accumulated sand from the north side of the pyramid. After much labour they found the entrance to a 'forced passage', probably made at the same time as the Great Pyramid was forced by al-Mamun. The condition of this passage was dangerous.

"I set a few men to work, but was convinced of the impossibility of advancing any further in that excavation. In the passage below, one of the men narrowly escaped being crushed to pieces. A large block of stone, no less than two metres long and 1.5 metres wide, fell from the top, while the man was digging beneath it. ... The man was imprisoned such that we had some difficulty in getting him out ... The falling of this stone had moved many others in this passage; indeed we were so situated that I thought it wise to retreat out of the pyramid... The danger was not only from what might fall upon us, but also what might fall in our way, close up the entrance, and thus bury us alive..."

After this setback, Belzoni examined the Second Pyramid again, and compared it with the Great Pyramid. He calculated that the entrance of Cheops's pyramid was not in the centre of the north face, but lay on the east side of the King's Chamber:

"The entrance consequently must be as far from the middle of the face as the distance from the centre of the chamber to the east side of it... Having made this clear and simple observation, I found that if there were any chambers at all in the Second Pyramid, the entrance could not be on the spot where I had excavated, which was in the centre, but calculated by the passage of the First Pyramid, the entrance to the second would be near 30 feet to the east. Satisfied with this calculation I appeared again at the Second Pyramid to examine the mass of rubbish. There was a little astonishment when I perceived the same marks which I had seen on the other spot in the centre, about thirty feet distant from where I stood. This gave me no little delight, and hope returned to my pyramidical brains."

Again the excavator summoned his peasants, who set to work murmuring "Magnoon!" which means crazy or mad in Arabic.

"The entry proved to be as hard as that of the first excavation, with this addition, that we found larger blocks of stone in our way, which had belonged to the pyramid beside the falling of the coating."

But hope rose on the 1st of March, when Belzoni discovered three blocks of granite, and on the following day :

Left: A view at the east face of the massive limestone blocks that form Chephren's pyramid core. The smooth blocks of Tura limestone that once covered the pyramid were removed in the Middle Ages. It still retains part of the limestone casing at its summit. The stones of Chephren's pyramid are roughly cut compared with Cheops's pyramid.

"We came at last to the right entrance into the pyramid... Having cleared the front of the three stones, the entrance proved to be a passage 1.2 metres high and a metre wide, formed of huge blocks of granite, which descended towards the centre for 31 metres at an angle of 26°."

At the bottom, a plug stone 37 centimetres thick barred their path.

"The raising of this was a work of no small consideration. The passage is only four feet high, and about a metre wide. Two men can't carry the stone and move... The only method was to raise it a little at a time... and at last we made the entrance large enough to squeeze myself in... After thirty days I had the pleasure to find myself in the way to the central chamber of one of the two great pyramids of Egypt."

After describing the entrance passage, Belzoni found himself in a horizontal one, cut out of the solid rock, which led to a large chamber.

"My torch, formed of a few wax candles, gave but a faint light. I could, however, distinguish clearly the principal objects. I naturally turned my eyes to the west end of the chamber looking for the sarcophagus, which I strongly expected to see in the same situation as that in the first pyramid; but I was disappointed when I saw nothing there... On my advancing towards the west end, however, I was agreeably surprised that there was a sarcophagus buried on a level with the floor. The sarcophagus contained nothing but rubbish and a few bones. On the walls of the chamber was an inscription in Arabic roughly written with charcoal. Translated it read: 'The Master Mohammed Ahmed has opened them; and the Master Osman attended this (opening) and the King Ali Mohammed at first (from the beginning) to the closing up'."

Belzoni found the tomb empty, as no doubt had the Arabs who preceded him centuries before, but his excavation measurement and description of the remaining passages were of no small value to Egyptology. As for the fragments of bones in the sarcophagus, Belzoni thought at first that they belonged to a human skeleton, but he adds, "Having been sent to London, they proved to be the bones of a bull."

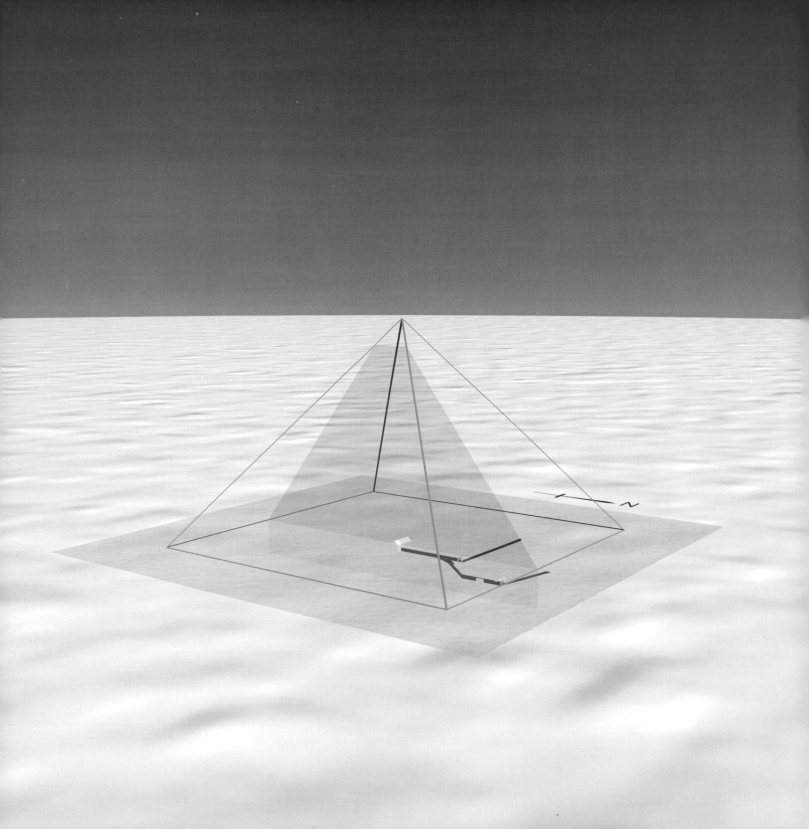

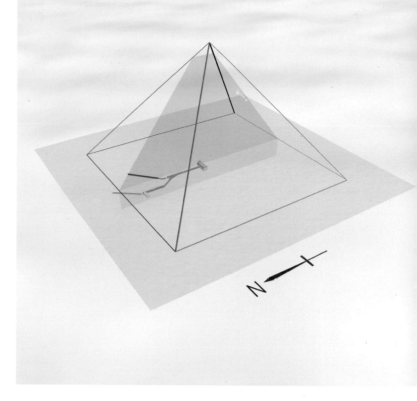

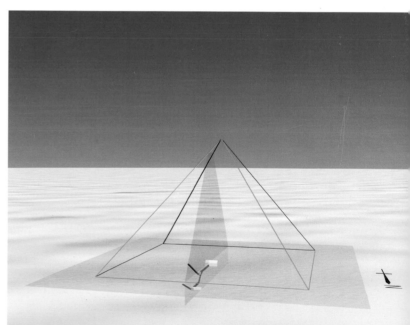

Inside the Pyramid of Chephren. The orange 'hyper plane' coincides with the entrance and descending passage. As in all other pyramids the entrance is from the northen face. It is displaced for 12m to the east from the centre of the northern face. The descending passage has a slope of 26°.

A modern, Sphinx-like Face

Left and previous pages: the magnificent diorite statue of Pharaoh Chephren is perhaps the finest Egyptian statue ever carved. The sculptor who carved and polished this statue did it with utmost care, showing he must have been skilled in many branches of knowledge. The hawk-god Horus is spreading his wings protectively around the Pharaoh's head expressing the ideal connection between earthly and divine power.

The modern Sphinx-like face is from *Egypt, Descriptive, Historical and Picturesque* by Professor Georg Ebers, Leipzig, 1879.

The Pyramid of Mycerinus

The third and smallest of the Giza group was built in *c.* 2500 BC by Menkeure (in Greek Mycerinus), the successor of the Pharaoh Chephren, and was known to the Egyptians as Neter-Menkeure, meaning 'Menkeure is Divine'. It follows the Pyramid of Chephren to the south-west. The vertical height is now 62m, having originally been 66m. Each side measures 108.5m and the slopes are 77m, originally 85m, at an angle of 51°. On the east side is the mortuary temple.

The Pharaoh died before his funerary temple was completed, and it was finished by his son Shepseskaf. More construction was carried out in the funerary complex in the Fifth and Sixth Dynasties. Herodotus wrote the following about Mycerinus: "The prince (Mycerinus) opposed his father's acts, reopened the temples, and allowed the miserable people to resume their ordinary life. His justice was beyond all other Pharaohs. He did not only give fair judgements, but if anyone was not satisfied with his sentence he compensated him from his own pocket, and thus pacified his anger."

George Reisner excavated the area around the valley temple, finding a large number of statues of the Pharaoh. Among the statues found are three magnificent triads showing the Pharaoh with the goddess Hathor and one of the nome deities. Mycerinus's intention was to have 42 of these statues, each representing him with one of the 42 deities. Only four were carved, three intact statues are in the Egyptian Museum, and the fourth was found in pieces. Also discovered in the valley building was a statue of Mycerinus and Queen Khamerenebti II, which had not been completely polished, possibly because of the Pharaoh's early death.

To the south of Menkaure's pyramid are three further satellite pyramids; all were found to be empty. This makes a total of ten pyramids at Giza, of which nine survive until today. If you want to photograph all nine pyramids together, take a camel or a horse ride towards the south-west until you reach a high plateau where you can picture all the pyramids in one frame (see pictures pages 16, 104 and 120).

Left: the pyramid of Mycerinus viewed from the south east and satellite pyramid in the foreground.
Right: the valley temple of Mycerinus.

Inside the Pyramid of Mycerinus

The passage (1) cut through the rock leads directly to the burial chamber. When this passage was abandoned due to the decision to increase the pyramid's size, another passage (3) was hewn in the rocks. The floor of the burial chamber was cut to a deeper level. Three blocking stones were placed between the Antechamber and the burial chamber. A second change of plan occurred, but here there was no decision to alter the pyramid's size. Two chambers (4) and (5) were hewn in the rocks, the latter being the new burial chamber and entirely built of granite. Its roof is a barrel-shaped vault. In this room, Colonel Howard Vyse found a magnificent sarcophagus with carved decorations. The body of Mycerinus must have been placed in this sarcophagus. Vyse took the sarcophagus, but while transporting it to England the vessel sank off the coast of Spain. In the first (2) burial chamber, Vyse found remains of human bones and a lid of a wooden anthropoid coffin with the name of Mycerinus carved on it (see picture page 145). These pieces are now in the British Museum. Carbon analyses of the bones showed that they belong to the Christian era. The type of carving on the wooden anthropoid shows that it belongs to the Saite period.

Left: the northern face of Mycerinus's pyramid, showing the modern staircase leading to the interior of the pyramid. The casing stone up to one third of the pyramid's height was made of granite. The first few rows are shown in the picture.

Top right: three satellite pyramids lie on the south side of the pyramid.

Right: the pair statue of Ramses II was discovered in 1996 by Zahi Hawass at the south-east corner of Mycerinus's pyramid. The statue represents Ramses II twice as a Pharaoh and as a deity. It is sculpted from a block of granite and was left unfinished because probably it was broken. It measures 3.4m in length and weighs 3.5 tons. This statue was made at the time of Ramses II i.e. 1,400 years after Mycerinus. The red granite was taken from the casing of the pyramid.

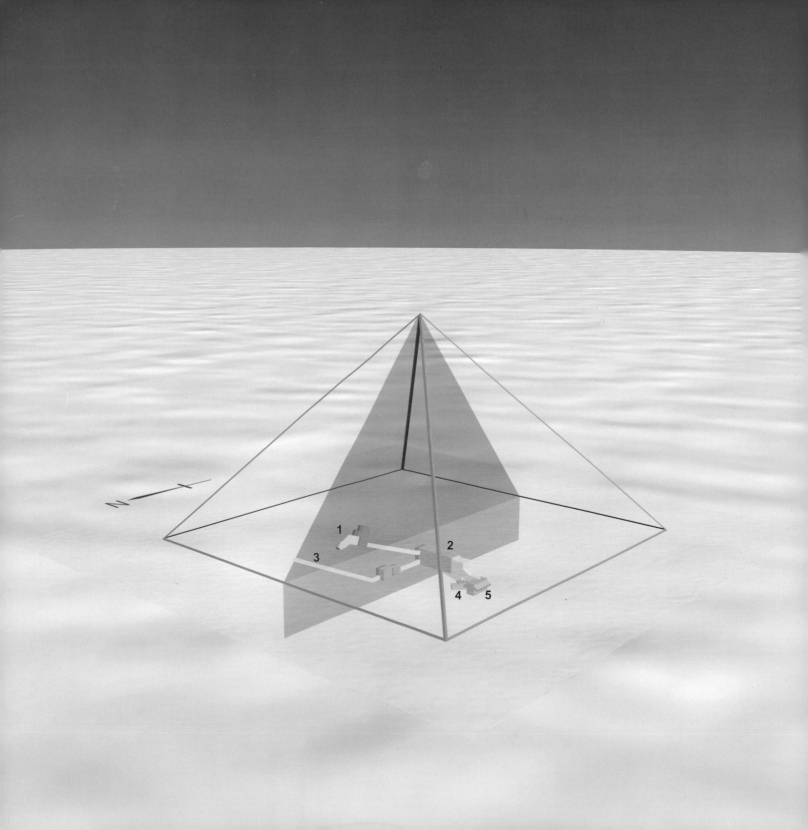

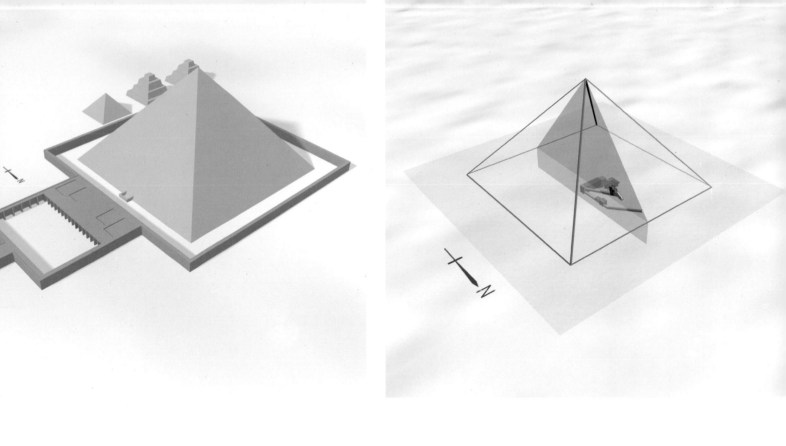

Left: inside the Pyramid of Mycerinus. The blue 'hyper plane' coincides with entrance passage which lies in the middle of the northern face. The light blue plane marks its extension below ground level.

1. Descending passage before increasing the pyramid's size.

2. Primitive burial chamber.

3. Descending passage.

4. Room with niches.

5. Burial chamber.

Above: a computer reconstruction of Mycerinus's pyramid.

50° 47′ 34″

66.5 m

108.5 m

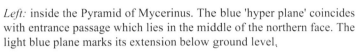

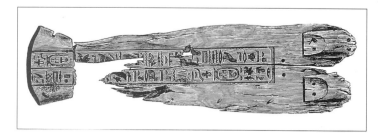

Left: looking west in the burial chamber (5).

Top: drawing of the burial chamber from *Egypt, Descriptive, Historical and Picturesque* by Georg Ebers, Leipzig, 1879. Note that the sarcophagus was still in its place.

Above: drawing of the remains of the wooden coffin from *Egypt, Descriptive, Historical and Picturesque* by Georg Ebers, Leipzig, 1879.

Top right: the descending passage (3).

Right: the primitive burial chamber (2) with stairs leading to burial chamber (5).

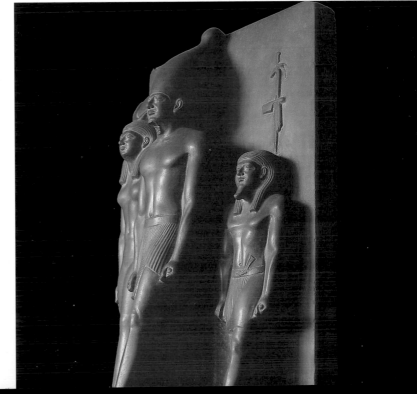

The Triad of Mycerinus

This is a group of three statues. In the centre is the Pharaoh Mycerinus wearing the White Crown of Upper Egypt. On his right stands goddess Hathor, goddess of the sky and of love. On her head she wears her characteristic emblem, the solar disk between two cow's horns. On Mycerinus's left side stands a different figure in each of the three statues.

Left and top right: on Mycerinus's left side stands a female figure personifying the cynopolite nome of Upper Egypt, Egyptian Museum.

Right: on Mycerinus's left side stands a male figure personifying the nome of Thebes, Egyptian Museum.

The Triad of Mycerinus

This is a group of three statues. In the centre is the Pharaoh Mycerinus wearing the White Crown of Upper Egypt. On his right stands the goddess Hathor, goddess of the sky and of love. On her head she wears her characteristic emblem, the solar disk between two cow's horns. On Mycerinus's left side stands a different figure in each of the three statues.

Left and right: on Mycerinus's left side stands a female figure personifying the Diospolis nome of Upper Egypt, Egyptian Museum.

Top right: on Mycerinus's left side stands a male figure personifying the nome of Thebes, Egyptian Museum.

The Great Sphinx, Horus in the Horizon

The Sphinx was chiselled from a limestone rock by Chephren, builder of the second Giza Pyramid. The Sphinx was probably conceived in three different stages. First, a foreman or artist noticed a projection of limestone hill in the quarried region to the south of the Pyramid of Cheops. Standing immediately to the north of Chephren's causeway and within a hundred metres of the valley temple, the small round hill impeded the view of Chephren's pyramid. It had to be levelled and its stone used for the hidden portions of Chephren's pyramid or it could be put to some other use.

The second intuition was that the rock resembled a lion. The third and peculiarly Egyptian intuition was to relate the lion to the Pharaoh whose pyramid complex was then under construction. This association had roots from far older times; pre-dynastic slate palettes show that the ruler could be represented as a lion. The lion not only symbolised power and might, he was also the supreme guardian. To the Ancient Egyptian, the lion was a dangerous animal. Sporting scenes from fifteen centuries after Chephren show that lions were a distinguished prey of the royal hunt. Representations of lions were also used in household furniture. His paws formed the feet of chairs; his body stretched out to form a bed. A tamed lion accompanied the Pharaoh into battle, representing the reassuring presence of a god. A lion is part of the divine; Sekhmet had a lioness' head. The lion was also linked with moisture: Tefnut was the lion-headed goddess of rain and dew. This association probably derived from the zodiacal sign of Leo, because it was in the summer time that the Nile began to flood. In Europe this concept is reflected in the continuous use of a lion's head as a waterspout.

After these intuitions came a third stage, the stage of accomplishment. Chephren's skilful masons transformed the ugly rock into a monument for their royal master. The body, with stretched paws and encircling tail, was 20m high and 72m long, with a nose almost as tall as a man and lips two metres long. The face is an idealised portrait of Chephren. The head has idealised features of Chephren wearing the customary cloth head-dress and with the Uraeus serpent on his brow. The Sphinx faces the rising sun.

Not all subsequent Egyptian sphinxes were male. A beardless female sphinx has been discovered at Abu Rawash. Later sphinxes are often difficult to date because a new ruler often ruined the stat-

The Great Sphinx guarding the Pyramid of Chephren. Carved *c.* 2500 BC by Pharaoh Chephren, it has become the emblem of Ancient and Modern Egypt.

ues of his predecessors. Some of the most interesting of these are the so-called Tanis sphinxes, in which only the mask is human while the ears of a lion replace human ears. Not all sphinxes had human face. Some had the head of a ram, the emblem of the god Amen-Re who was to dominate the last thousand years of Ancient Egyptian history. An avenue of such sphinxes survives outside the great temple at Karnak. During the New Kingdom, the Great Sphinx was a centre of a special cult and became a symbol of the sun-god.

Dream Stelae. The Pharaoh Amenhotep II of the XVIIIth Dynasty was succeeded by his young son, Tuthmosis IV (1419 - 1386 BC). One of the principal events in the Pharaoh's reign was the excavation of the Great Sphinx from the drifting desert sand, which had covered it up to its neck. How the impulse to liberate the Sphinx from the drifting sand came to Tuthmosis IV is described by the Pharaoh himself on a monument which he ordered to be installed between the forepaw of the colossal figure. According to this inscription, before his accession to the throne Tuthmosis IV frequently entertained himself as a young prince by desert hunts in the vicinity of Memphis. He drove his chariot "whose horses were swifter than the wind" while killing lions and gazelles with his spear. On one of these hunting excursions the prince seated himself during the heat of the day in the "shadow of this great god". At the moment when the sun reached its highest point in the sky, he fell asleep in the shadow of the Sphinx, who spoke to him with his own mouth, as a father speaks to his son.

The Great Sphinx

This is the largest piece of sculpture ever carved by man. The Ancient Egyptians recognized in the Sphinx the sun-god, and called it therefore *Harmachis Horus*, "Horus on the Horizon". The word sphinx is a distorted Greek translation of the Egyptian word shesep-ankh, living image".

Although *c.* 4,500 years old, only during the 19th century has the Sphinx been compelled to reveal its lion-body and stand naked to light.

The height from the ground to the top of the head is 20m and the length from the front paws to the tail is 73m; the greatest width of the face is four metres. The ear measures 1.37m and the mouth two metres. The nose is estimated to have been 1.14m long.

Page 155: of the original dark red colour of the face only slight traces remain. Clearly visible is the missing nose and the intentional destruction on the face. Every time I had a close look at the Sphinx's face I asked myself: "Why is it that men are so ready to destroy the works of man". The destroyers have dreamed of sweeping the Sphinx away from the face of the earth. From the chin once hung a long beared, fragments of which were found by Napoleon. Later it was given to the British.

"Look upon me and behold me! O my son, I am your father, I shall give to you my reign upon earth over the living and you shall wear its red crown and its white crown on the throne of Geb the prince. To you shall belong the earth in its length and its breadth, together with that which the eye of the All-Lord illuminates, and to you shall be apportioned the nourishment of ... the Two Lands and the great tribute of every foreign country. For prolonged years already my face has been turned to you and my heart likewise. You shall be to me one to carry out my will, in as much as I am suffering in all my perfect body. For the sand of this desert on which I am is pressing me. Hasten to me to do what is in my heart; for I know that you are my son and my champion. Approach; I am with you; I am your guide."

When Tuthmosis awoke, he was still conscious of the words of the god, and they remained in his memory until his accession to the throne. Immediately upon the beginning of his reign, he fulfilled the request of the Sphinx who had given him sovereignty, and ordered the removal of the sand which had almost buried the Sphinx. Again in 1926, the Egyptian Antiquities Department had to free the Sphinx once more from the encroaching sands.

Suggested Reading

A History of Ancient Egypt, Nicolas Grimal, Blackwell Publishers Ltd., 1992.

Ancient Egypt, General Editor: David Silverman, Duncan Baird Publishers Ltd., 1997.

Chronicle of the Pharaohs, Peter A. Clayton, Thames and Hudson Ltd., London, 1994.

Die Ägyptische Pyramiden: vom Ziegelbau zum Weltwunder, Rainer Stadelmann, Mainz 1985.

Egypt to the end of the Old Kingdom, Cyril Alfred, Thames and Hudson, 1988.

Genie et démesure d'un Pharaon: KHÉOPS; Jean Kersil, Paris 1996.

In the Shadow of the pyramidions, Jaromir Malek, AUC Book Press in Cairo, 1986.

Pharaohs and Pyramids, Georg Heart, The Herbert Press, London, 1991.

Sakkara and Memphis, Jill Kamil, Egyptian International Publishing Company, 1978.

The Complete Pyramids, Mark Lehner, Thames and Hudson Ltd., London, 1997.

The Pyramids, Ahmed Fakhry, The University of Chicago Press, 1961.

The Pyramids, Miroslav Verner, AUC Book Press Cairo, 1997.

The Pyramids of Egypt, Edwards I. E. S., London 1965.

The Rhind Mathematical Papyrus, Gay Robins & Charles Shute, British Museum Publications, 1987.

Equipment

I photographed all pictures of this book with my Hasselblad. For wide angle pictures I used the Hasselblad SWC/M with the Biogon 38 mm lens. For the other pictures I used the Hasselblad 500CM and 501CM with the normal Planar 80 mm lens, Planar 100 mm, the Makro Planar 120 mm lens, the Sonar 150 mm lens, the Super Achromat 250 mm lens, and the Tele Tessar 500 mm lens. And the Provia 100 ASA film has been used in all cases.

The various stages of printing were carried out at my printing press 'Farid Atiya Press.' Colour separation and image setting we did with the 'superb' Hell drum scanner. This heavy duty classical machine gave excellent results, and cannot be compared with the new 'table top' machines. The offset printing we did with a Heidelberg SORSZ machine. Folding we did with a Stahl K78 machine. Hartmann printing ink and varnish were used as well as Kodak Polychrome image setting films and printing plates.